C000299393

FOOD FOR THE JOURNEY

A Spiritual Companion
on Becoming a Catholic

All documents are published
thanks to the generous support of the members
of the Catholic Truth Society

CATHOLIC TRUTH SOCIETY
PUBLISHERS TO THE HOLY SEE

FOOD FOR THE JOURNEY

A Spiritual Companion
on Becoming a Catholic

Contents

5

6

BASIC PRAYERS

Our Father

Our Father, who art in heaven,
hallowed be thy name.
Thy Kingdom come.
Thy will be done on earth as it is in heaven.
Give us this day our daily bread,
and forgive us our trespasses,
as we forgive those who trespass against us,
and lead us not into temptation,
but deliver us from evil.
Amen.

Hail Mary

Hail, Mary, full of grace, the Lord is with thee.
Blessed art thou among women,
and blessed is the fruit of thy womb, Jesus.
Holy Mary, Mother of God,
pray for us sinners,
now, and at the hour of our death.
Amen.

Glory be to the Father

Glory be to the Father,
and to the Son,
and to the Holy Spirit.
As it was in the beginning,
is now, and ever shall be,
world without end.
Amen.

I Believe (The Apostles' Creed)

I believe in God,
the Father almighty,
Creator of heaven and earth,
and in Jesus Christ, his only Son, our Lord,
who was conceived by the Holy Spirit,
born of the Virgin Mary,
suffered under Pontius Pilate,
was crucified, died and was buried;
he descended into hell;
on the third day he rose again from the dead;
he ascended into heaven,
and is seated at the right hand of God
    the Father almighty;
from there he will come to judge the living
    and the dead.
I believe in the Holy Spirit,
the holy Catholic Church,
the communion of saints,
the forgiveness of sins,
the resurrection of the body,
and life everlasting.
Amen.

Act of Faith

My God,
I believe in you and all that your Church teaches,
because you have said it,
and your word is true.

Act of Hope

My God,
I hope in you,
for grace and for glory,
because of your promises,
your mercy and your power.

Act of Charity

My God,
because you are so good,
I love you with all my heart,
and for your sake,
I love my neighbour as myself.

Commendation

Jesus, Mary and Joseph,
I give you my heart and my soul.

Jesus, Mary and Joseph,
assist me in my last agony.

Jesus, Mary and Joseph,
may I breathe forth my soul in peace with you.

Act of Resignation

O Lord, my God
whatever manner of death is pleasing to you,
with all its anguish, pains and sorrows,
I now accept from your hand with a resigned
   and willing spirit.

For the Faithful Departed

Out of the depths I cry to you, O Lord,
Lord hear my voice!
O let your ears be attentive
to the voice of my pleading.

If you, O Lord, should mark our guilt,
Lord, who would survive?
But with you is found forgiveness:
for this we revere you.

My soul is waiting for the Lord,
I count on his word.
My soul is longing for the Lord
more than watchmen for daybreak.
Let the watchman count on daybreak
and Israel on the Lord.

Because with the Lord there is mercy
and fullness of redemption;
Israel indeed he will redeem
from all its iniquity.

(*Psalm* 130)

V.   Eternal rest grant to them, O Lord.
R.   And let perpetual light shine upon them.
V.   May they rest in peace.
R.   Amen.

Let us pray:

O God, the Creator and Redeemer of all the faithful,
grant to the souls of your servants departed
the remission of all their sins,
that through our pious supplication
they may obtain that pardon which
    they have always desired;
who live and reign for ever and ever.
R. Amen.

For help

May the divine assistance remain always with us
✠ and may the souls of the faithful departed,
through the mercy of God, rest in peace.
Amen.

Prayer before a Crucifix

Behold, O kind and most sweet Jesus,
I cast myself on my knees in your sight,
and with the most fervent desire of my soul,
I pray and beseech you
that you would impress upon my heart
lively sentiments of faith, hope, and charity,
with a true repentance for my sins,
and a firm desire of amendment,
while with deep affection and grief of soul
I ponder within myself and mentally contemplate
    your five most precious wounds;
having before my eyes that which David spoke
    in prophecy of you,
O good Jesus: "They pierced my hands and my feet;
they have numbered all my bones".

MORNING &
EVENING PRAYER

Morning Prayer

V.   Lord, open our lips.
R.   And we shall praise your name.
Glory be to the Father... (Alleluia)

A hymn, suitable to the time of day or feast, may follow.

Psalm 99

(This or alternative psalms may be said)

Cry out with joy to the Lord, all the earth
Serve the Lord with gladness.
Come before him, singing for joy.

Know that he, the Lord, is God.
He made us, we belong to him,
We are the people, the sheep of his flock.

Go within his gates, giving thanks.
Enter his courts with songs of praise.
Give thanks to him and bless his name.

Indeed, how good is the Lord,
Eternal his merciful love.
He is faithful from age to age.
Glory be to the Father...

Scripture

(An alternative passage may be used)

You know what hour it is, how it is full time now for you to wake from sleep. The night is far gone, the day is at hand. Let us cast off the works of darkness and put on the armour of light; let us conduct ourselves becomingly as in the day. (*Romans* 13:11-13)

The Benedictus (Luke 1:68-79)

Blessed be the Lord, the God of Israel!
He has visited his people and redeemed them.
He has raised up for us a mighty saviour
in the house of David his servant,
as he promised by the lips of holy men,
those who were his prophets from of old.
A saviour who would free us from our foes,
from the hands of all who hate us.
So his love for our fathers is fulfilled
and his holy covenant remembered.
He swore to Abraham our father to grant us,
that free from fear, and saved from the hands
    of our foes,
we might serve him in holiness and justice
all the days of our life in his presence.
As for you, little child,
you shall be called a prophet of God, the Most High.
You shall go ahead of the Lord
to prepare a way for him,
To make known to his people their salvation
 through forgiveness of all their sins,
the loving kindness of the heart of our God
who visits us like the dawn from on high.
He will give light to those in darkness,
those who dwell in the shadow of death,
and guide us into the way of peace.
Glory be to the Father…

Intercessions

(These or other intercessions may be used)

Let us pray to Christ our Lord,
the sun who enlightens all people -
Lord our Saviour, give us life!
(may be repeated after each line)
We thank you for the gift of this new day -
May your Holy Spirit guide us to do your will -
Help us to manifest your love to all those we meet -
Renew in us your gifts -
May we go forth in peace -
Our Father…

Concluding prayer

Almighty God, you have given us this day; strengthen
us with your power
and keep us from falling into sin,
so that whatever we say, or think, or do,
may be in your service and for the sake of the kingdom.
We ask this through Christ our Lord.
Amen.

✠ The Lord bless us, keep us from all evil and bring us
to everlasting life.
Amen.

Alternative personal prayers may include:

Our Father. Hail Mary. Glory be. I Believe.

Offering

O my God, I offer you all my thoughts,
words, actions, and sufferings;
and I beseech you to give me your grace
that I may not offend you this day,
but may faithfully serve you and do your holy will
  in all things.
I entrust myself completely to your boundless mercy
  today and always.

O Lord you have brought me to the beginning
of a new day.
Save me by your power so that I may not fall
  into any sin.
May everything I say, and all that I do,
be directed to the performance of your justice,
through Christ our Lord.

L ord, may everything I do begin with your
inspiration, continue with your help
and reach conclusion under your guidance.

Morning offering

O Jesus, through the most pure heart of Mary,
I offer you all my prayers, thoughts,
works and sufferings of this day
for all the intentions of your most Sacred Heart.

O most Sacred Heart of Jesus, I place all my trust in you.

O most Sacred Heart of Jesus, I place all my trust in you.

O most Sacred Heart of Jesus, I place all my trust in you.

During the Day

The Angelus

May be said morning, noon, and night, to put us in mind that God the Son became man for our salvation.

V. The Angel of the Lord declared to Mary:
R. And she conceived of the Holy Spirit.
    Hail Mary…

V. Behold the handmaid of the Lord:
R. Be it done to me according to your word.
    Hail Mary…

V. And the Word was made flesh:
R. And dwelt among us.
    Hail Mary…

V. Pray for us, O holy Mother of God.
R. That we may be made worthy of the promises of Christ.

Let us pray:

Pour forth, we beseech you, O Lord,
   your grace into our hearts,
that we, to whom the Incarnation of Christ,
   your Son,
was made known by the message of an Angel,
may by his Passion and Cross ✠
be brought to the glory of his Resurrection,
through the same Christ our Lord.
R. Amen.

(In Eastertime, the Angelus is replaced by the Regina Caeli)

V.   O God, come to our aid.
R.   O Lord, make haste to help us.
Glory be to the Father…

Hymn

A hymn, suitable to the time of day or feast, may follow, e.g.:

O Trinity of blessed light,
O Unity of princely might,
The fiery sun now goes his way;
Shed thou within our hearts thy ray.
To thee our morning song of praise,
To thee our evening prayer we raise;
Thy glory suppliant we adore
For ever and for evermore.
All laud to God the Father be;
All praise, eternal Son, to thee;
All glory, as is ever meet,
To God the holy Paraclete.
Amen.

25

Psalm 16

(An alternative psalm may be said)

Preserve me, God, I take refuge in you.
I say to the Lord: "You are my God.
My happiness lies in you alone".

He has put into my heart a marvellous love
for the faithful ones who dwell in his land.
Those who choose other gods increase their sorrows.
Never will I offer their offerings of blood.
Never will I take their name upon my lips.

O Lord, it is you who are my portion and cup;
it is you yourself who are my prize.
The lot marked out for me is my delight:
welcome indeed the heritage that falls to me!

I will bless the Lord who gives me counsel,
who even at night directs my heart.
I keep the Lord ever in my sight:
since he is at my right hand, I shall stand firm.

And so my heart rejoices, my soul is glad;
even my body shall rest in safety.
For you will not leave my soul among the dead,
nor let your beloved know decay.

You will show me the path of life,
the fullness of joy in your presence,
at your right hand happiness for ever.
Glory be to the Father…

Scripture

(An alternative passage may be used)

Let us give thanks to the God and Father of our Lord Jesus Christ, the merciful Father, the God from whom all help comes! He helps us in all our troubles, so that we are able to help those who have all kinds of troubles, using the same help that we ourselves have received from God. (*2 Corinthians* 1:3-4)

Magnificat (Luke 1:46-55)

My soul glorifies the Lord,
my spirit rejoices in God, my Saviour.
He looks on his servant in her lowliness; henceforth all ages will call me blessed.
The Almighty works marvels for me.
Holy his name!
His mercy is from age to age,
on those who fear him.
He puts forth his arm in strength
and scatters the proud-hearted.
He casts the mighty from their thrones
and raises the lowly.
He fills the starving with good things,
sends the rich away empty.
He protects Israel, his servant,
remembering his mercy,
the mercy promised to our fathers,
to Abraham and his sons for ever.
Glory be to the Father…

Intercessions

(These or other intercessions may be used)

May your kingdom of peace and justice
be realised on earth as in heaven -
Lord, hear our prayer.
(may be repeated after each line)

Show yourself to all who seek you
in sincerity of heart -

Lord Jesus Christ,
light of all the nations,
shine upon those who walk in darkness
and in the shadow of death -

Be with all those who suffer in mind,
body or spirit -

Show mercy to the dead;
bring them to rejoice in the company
of the Blessed Virgin Mary
and all your saints -

Our Father…

Concluding prayer

Let our evening prayer rise before you
like incense, Lord, and may your blessing
shower down upon us: so that now and for ever your
grace may heal and save us.
We ask this through Christ Our Lord.
Amen.
✠ May the Lord bless us, keep us from all evil
and bring us to everlasting life.

Alternative personal prayers may include:
Our Father. Hail Mary. Glory be. I Believe.

O my God, I thank you for all the benefits
which I have ever received from you,
and especially this day.
Give me light to see what sins I have committed,
and grant me the grace to be truly sorry for them.
(A brief examination of conscience may follow)

O my God, because you are so good,
I am very sorry that I have sinned against you
and by the help of your grace I will not sin again.

On going to bed

Into your hands, O Lord, I commend my spirit:
Lord Jesus, receive my soul.
In the name of our Lord Jesus Christ crucified,
I lay me down to rest.
Bless me, O Lord, and defend me;
preserve me from a sudden and unprovided death
and from all dangers,
and bring me to life everlasting with you.

PRAYERS TO
THE HOLY SPIRIT

Veni Creator Spiritus

Come, Holy Spirit, Creator, come
from thy bright heavenly throne.
Come, take possession of our souls,
and make them all thine own.

Thou who art called the Paraclete,
best gift of God above,
the living spring, the living fire,
sweet unction and true love.

Thou who art sevenfold in thy grace,
finger of God's right hand;
his promise, teaching little ones
to speak and understand.

O guide our minds with thy blest light,
with love our hearts inflame;
and with thy strength which never decays,
confirm our mortal frame.

Far from us drive our deadly foe;
true peace unto us bring;
and through all perils lead us safe
beneath thy sacred wing.

Through thee may we the Father know,
through thee the eternal Son,
and thee, the Spirit of them both,
thrice-blessed Three in One.

All glory to the Father be,
with his co-equal Son;
the same to thee, great Paraclete,
while endless ages run.

Veni Sancte Spiritus

Come, Holy Spirit, come!
And from your celestial home
Shed a ray of light divine!

Come, Father of the poor!
Come, source of all our store!
Come, within our bosoms shine.

You, of comforters the best;
You, the soul's most welcome guest;
Sweet refreshment here below.

In our labour, rest most sweet;
Grateful coolness in the heat;
Solace in the midst of woe.

O most blessed Light divine,
Shine within these hearts of yours,
And our inmost being fill!

Where you are not, we have naught,
Nothing good in deed or thought,
Nothing free from taint of ill.

Heal our wounds, our strength renew;
On our dryness pour your dew;
Wash the stains of guilt away.

Bend the stubborn heart and will;
Melt the frozen, warm the chill;
Guide the steps that go astray.

On the faithful, who adore
And confess you, evermore
In your sevenfold gift descend.

Give them virtue's sure reward;
Give them your salvation, Lord;
Give them joys that never end.
Amen.

Prayer to the Holy Spirit

V.   Come, O Holy Spirit,
       fill the hearts of your faithful,

R.   and enkindle in them the fire of your love.

V.   Send forth your Spirit and they shall
       be created.

R.   And you shall renew the face of the earth.

Let us pray:

O God, who taught the hearts of the faithful
by the light of the Holy Spirit,
grant that by the gift of the same Spirit
we may be always truly wise and ever rejoice
   in his consolation.
Through Christ our Lord.
R. Amen.

PENITENTIAL
PRAYERS

Sacrament of Reconciliation

Remember that the sacrament is above all an act of God's love. It is a personal moment to be lived in a relationship of love with God. It is not routine, nor an ordeal to be gone through, but is very much part of the personal renewal which takes place in each person. You are invited, in the light of God's love, to recognise the sinfulness of your life, to have true sorrow for your sins, and a firm intention to avoid them in future.

Essential elements of a good confession

To make a good confession, we should:

1. Pray first, asking God to help us.

2. Make a sincere examination of conscience to see how we have sinned since our last confession.

3. Confess our sins simply, with humility and honesty.

4. Make our act of contrition with heartfelt sorrow and a "firm purpose of amendment", being determined that we will avoid the occasions of sin.

5. Devoutly carry out the penance prescribed and pray in thanksgiving for God's overflowing love and mercy.

Prayer before Confession

Almighty and merciful God,
you have brought me here in the name of
your Son to receive your mercy and grace
in my time of need.
Open my eyes to see the evil I have done.
Touch my heart and convert me to yourself.
Where sin has separated me from you,
may your love unite me to you again:
where sin has brought weakness,
may your power heal and strengthen;
where sin has brought death,
may your Spirit raise to new life.
Give me a new heart to love you,
so that my life may reflect the image of your Son.
May the world see the glory of Christ
    revealed in your Church,
and come to know that he is the one
    whom you have sent,
Jesus Christ, your Son, our Lord.
Amen.

The Confiteor

I confess to almighty God
and to you, my brothers and sisters,
that I have greatly sinned,
in my thoughts and in my words,
in what I have done and in what I have failed to do,
through my fault, through my fault,
through my most grievous fault;
therefore I ask blessed Mary ever-Virgin,
all the Angels and Saints,
and you, my brothers and sisters,
to pray for me to the Lord our God.

An Act of Contrition

O my God, I am sorry and beg pardon for all my sins,
and detest them above all things,
because they deserve your dreadful punishments,
because they have crucified
my loving Saviour Jesus Christ, and, most of all,
because they offend your infinite goodness;
and I firmly resolve, by the help of your grace,
never to offend you again,
and carefully to avoid the occasions of sin.

Examination of Conscience

Careful preparation is vital in order to make the most of this encounter with our loving heavenly Father. Find some time to be alone and quiet to reflect on your life, your relationship with God and others. An examination of conscience provides us with what we are going to say in the confessional. Without time given to such examination our confession is in danger of being incomplete. There are many ways: one is to use a Gospel passage, especially one of the many healing miracles or occasions of forgiveness (e.g. *Luke* 15:11-32; *John* 4:5-42; *Matthew* 18:21-35; *Luke* 18:9-14). Imagine you are the person being healed or forgiven by Jesus. Read the Scripture passage, imagine you are in the scene, and listen to the words of Jesus. He speaks to you! What do you say? Alternatively, Jesus summed up and extended the Ten Commandments by his two great commandments (*Mark* 12:28-42): love God and your neighbour.

Mortal sin is sin whose object is a grave matter and which is also committed with full knowledge and deliberate consent (*Catechism* 1857). We must confess all mortal sins. We are not obliged to confess all venial sins. We commit venial sin when, in a less serious matter, we do not observe the standard prescribed by the moral law, or when we disobey the moral law in a grave matter, but without full knowledge or without complete consent (*Catechism* 1862). Confession of venial sins is an act of devotion. We need not be unduly anxious to confess them all, but may rather choose to focus on areas of our life that are most in need of God's grace.

The following examination of conscience can help us to measure our lives by the objective standard of Christ's teaching. We may also consider more generally how we may have failed in our lives to live fully as Disciples of Christ.

Sins against God

- Have I rejected my faith, refused to find out more about it?

- Have I forgotten my daily prayers or said them badly?

- Have I experimented with the occult or put my trust in fortune tellers or horoscopes?

- Have I blasphemed against God or used bad language?

- Have I shown disrespect for holy things, places or people?

- Have I missed Mass on Sundays or Holydays through my own fault?

- Have I let myself be distracted at Mass or distracted others?

- Have I received Holy Communion in a state of mortal sin?

- Have I received Holy Communion without proper reverence, care or thanksgiving?

Sins against myself and others

- Have I been impatient, angry or jealous?

- Have I brooded over injuries or refused to forgive?

- Have I taken part in or encouraged abortion, the destruction of human embryos, euthanasia or any other means of taking human life?

- Have I been verbally or physically violent to others?

- Have I been racist in my thoughts, words or deeds?

- Have I hurt anyone by speaking badly about them?

- Have I betrayed confidences without good cause or revealed things simply to hurt others?

- Have I judged others rashly?

- Have I been drunk or used illegal drugs?

- Have I driven dangerously or inconsiderately?

- Have I spoken in an obscene way?

- Have I looked at obscene pictures, films or books?

- Have I been involved in any impure behaviour on my own or with someone else?

- Have I been vain, proud, selfish or self-seeking?

- Have I told lies to excuse myself, to hurt others or to make myself look more important?

- Have I stolen anything?

- Have I failed to contribute to the support of the Church in proportion to my means?

- Have I been disobedient, rude or insolent to those in authority over me?

- Have I been harsh, overbearing or sarcastic to those under my authority?

- Have I cheated my employers or employees?

- Have I misused or damaged the property of others?

- Have I set my heart greedily on possessing things?

- Have I given scandal or bad example?

- Have I been lazy at my work, study or domestic duties?

- Have I been jealous of others - of their looks, their popularity, their good work?

- Have I encouraged others to do wrong in any way?

For spouses

- Have I neglected to foster the warmth of my love and affection for my spouse?

- Have I prolonged disagreements through resentment or failing to apologise when I have been in the wrong?

- Have I mistreated my spouse verbally, emotionally or physically?

- Have I used artificial means of birth control?

- Have I been unfaithful to my spouse in any way?

For parents

- Have I neglected to teach my children to pray?

- Have I neglected the religious education of my children?

- Have I failed to bring my children to Sunday Mass?

- Have I argued with my spouse in front of my children?

- Have I failed to exercise vigilance over what my children read, see on television or on the internet?

- Have I been harsh or overbearing to my children?

- Have I neglected my children's welfare in any way?

For young people

- Have I been disobedient to my parents?

- Have I been unhelpful at home?

- Have I failed to try to understand my parents and talk with them?

- Have I upset the peace of my home for selfish reasons?

- Have I lost control when I have been angry?

- Have I sulked or been sarcastic instead of asking for help?

- Have I failed to work properly at school?

- Have I treated teachers or other adults with disrespect?

- Have I played unfairly at games or sports?

- Have I taken part in fights?

Going to Confession

(You may take this prayer book with you to Confession)

Reception

The priest welcomes the penitent warmly.
The penitent and priest begin by making the Sign of
the Cross, while saying:

✠ In the name of the Father,
and of the Son,
and of the Holy Spirit.
Amen.

The priest invites you to trust in God. You may indicate your
state of life, and anything else which may help the priest
as confessor.

The Word of God

The priest may invite you to reflect on a passage from Holy
Scripture, speaking of God's mercy and call to conversion.

Reconciliation

Then you can speak in your own words or you can say:

Bless me Father for I have sinned.
My last confession was … ago
(say roughly how long)
and these are my sins.

Now tell your sins simply in your own words.
When you have finished, let the priest know.
You can use these words if you wish:
I am sorry for all these sins and for any that I cannot
now remember.

Listen carefully to the advice of the priest and ask the Holy Spirit to help him to say what is best to help you to grow in the Christian life. You can ask him questions if you want. The priest may propose an Act of Penance, which should serve not only to make up for the past but also to help begin a new life and provide an antidote to weakness. It may take the form of prayer, self-denial, and especially of service to one's neighbour and works of mercy.

Then the priest invites you to say a prayer of sorrow (an *Act of Contrition*), such as:

O my God, because you are so good,
I am very sorry that I have sinned against you,
and by the help of your grace I will not sin again.

Wait while the priest says the prayer of "Absolution" (where Christ forgives you all your sins).

Make the Sign of the Cross as the priest says:

I absolve you from your sins
in the name of the Father,
and of the Son, ✠ and of the Holy Spirit.
Amen.

The priest may say a few final words of encouragement to you as you leave.

After Confession

Take some time in the quiet of the Church to reflect on the grace of the sacrament and to thank God for his mercy and forgiveness. Here is a prayer of thanksgiving:

Father, in your love you have brought me from
evil to good and from misery to happiness. Through
your blessings give me the courage
of perseverance.
Amen.

The Way of the Cross

The Way of the Cross is a devotion to the Sacred Passion in which we accompany, in spirit, our Blessed Lord in his sorrowful journey from the house of Pilate to Calvary, and recall, with sorrow and love, all that took place from the time when he was condemned to death to his being laid in the tomb. We meditate devoutly on the Passion and Death of our Lord as we move around the stations in the Church.

Often, when made publicly, the following response is said at each station as we genuflect:

V. We adore you, O Christ, and we praise you.

R. Because by your Holy Cross you have redeemed the world.

The following act of contrition may be used at each station:

I love you, Jesus, my love above all things.
I repent with my whole heart of having offended you.
Never permit me to separate myself from you again.
Grant that I may love you always
and then do with me what you will.

Our Father; Hail Mary; Glory be.

I. Jesus is condemned to death

Consider how Jesus, after having been scourged and crowned with thorns, was unjustly condemned by Pilate to die on the Cross.

II. Jesus receives the Cross

Consider how Jesus, in making this journey with the Cross on his shoulders, thought of us, and offered for us to his Father the death he was about to undergo.

III. Jesus falls the first time

Consider the first fall of Jesus under his Cross. His flesh was torn by the scourges, his head was crowned with thorns; he had lost a great quantity of blood. So weakened he could scarcely walk, he yet had to carry this great load upon his shoulders. The soldiers struck him rudely, and he fell several times.

IV. Jesus is met by his Blessed Mother

Consider this meeting of the Son and the Mother, which took place on this journey. Their looks became like so many arrows to wound those hearts which loved each other so tenderly.

V. The Cross is laid upon Simon of Cyrene

Consider how his cruel tormentors, seeing that Jesus was on the point of expiring, and fearing he would die on the way, whereas they wished him to die the shameful death of the Cross, constrained Simon of Cyrene to carry the Cross behind our Lord.

VI. Veronica wipes the face of Jesus

Consider how the holy woman named Veronica, seeing Jesus so ill-used, and bathed in sweat and blood, wiped his face with a towel, on which was left the impression of his holy countenance.

VII. Jesus falls the second time

Consider the second fall of Jesus under the Cross; a fall which renews the pain of all the wounds in his head and members.

VIII. The women of Jerusalem mourn for our Lord

Consider how these women wept with compassion at seeing Jesus in such a pitiable state, streaming with blood, as he walked along. "Daughters of Jerusalem", said he, "weep not for me, but for yourselves and for your children".

IX. Jesus falls the third time

Consider the third fall of Jesus Christ. His weakness was extreme, and the cruelty of his executioners excessive, who tried to hasten his steps when he could scarcely move.

X. Jesus is stripped of his garments

Consider the violence with which Jesus was stripped by the executioners. His inner garments adhered to his torn flesh, and they dragged them off so roughly that the skin came with them. Take pity on your Saviour thus cruelly treated.

XI. Jesus is nailed to the Cross

Consider how Jesus, having been placed upon the Cross, extended his hands, and offered to his Eternal Father the sacrifice of his life for our salvation. Those barbarians fastened him with nails, and then, securing the Cross, allowed him to die with anguish on this infamous gibbet.

XII. Jesus dies on the Cross

Consider how Jesus, being consumed with anguish after three hours' agony on the Cross, abandoned himself to the weight of his body, bowed his head and died.

XIII. Jesus is taken down from the Cross

Consider how, after our Lord had expired, two of his disciples, Joseph and Nicodemus, took him down from the Cross and placed him in the arms of his afflicted Mother, who received him with unutterable tenderness, and pressed him to her bosom.

XIV. Jesus is placed in the sepulchre

Consider how the disciples, accompanied by his holy Mother, carried the body of Jesus to bury it. They closed the tomb, and all came sorrowfully away.

DEVOTIONAL
PRAYERS OF
THE CHURCH

The Divine Mercy

The devotion consists in the adoration of Mercy, the heart of which is trust, meaning to assume an attitude conforming to Jesus's will. Trustful believers are assured many graces in this world and eternal happiness in the next. The Novena of the Divine Mercy (which includes the Chaplet, and other prayers) begins on Good Friday and ends on Divine Mercy Sunday.

The Chaplet

Prayed on ordinary rosary beads, in the following order:

The Our Father, Hail Mary, Apostles' Creed.

On the large bead before each decade:

Eternal Father,
I offer you the Body and Blood,
Soul and Divinity of Your dearly beloved Son,
Our Lord Jesus Christ,
in atonement for our sins and those of the world.

Once on each of the ten small beads:

For the sake of his sorrowful Passion,
have mercy on us and on the whole world.

Concluding doxology

After five decades repeat three times:

Holy God, Holy Mighty One, Holy Immortal One,
have mercy on us and the whole world.

O Blood and Water

O Blood and Water, which gushed forth from the heart of Jesus as a Fount of Mercy for us, I trust in you.

The Litany of the Divine Mercy

Divine Mercy,
gushing forth from the bosom of the Father,
I trust in you. (Repeat this after each line)

Divine Mercy, greatest attribute of God,

Divine Mercy, incomprehensible mystery,

Divine Mercy, fountain gushing forth from the mystery
of the Most Blessed Trinity,

Divine Mercy, unfathomed by any intellect,
human or angelic,

Divine Mercy, from which wells forth all life
and happiness,

Divine Mercy, better than the heavens,

Divine Mercy, source of miracles and wonders,

Divine Mercy, encompassing the whole universe,

Divine Mercy, descending to earth in the Person
of the Incarnate Word,

Divine Mercy, which flowed out from the open wound
of the Heart of Jesus,

Divine Mercy, enclosed in the Heart of Jesus for us,
and especially for sinners,

Divine Mercy, unfathomed in the institution of
the Sacred Heart,

Divine Mercy, in the founding of Holy Church,

Divine Mercy, in the Sacrament of Holy Baptism,

Divine Mercy, in our justification through Jesus Christ,

Divine Mercy, accompanying us through our whole life,

Divine Mercy, embracing us
especially at the hour of death,

Divine Mercy, endowing us with immortal life,

Divine Mercy, accompanying us
every moment of our life,

Divine Mercy, shielding us from the fire of hell,

Divine Mercy, in the conversion of hardened sinners,

Divine Mercy, astonishment for Angels,
incomprehensible to Saints,

Divine Mercy, unfathomed in all the mysteries of God,

Divine Mercy, lifting us out of every misery,

Divine Mercy, source of our happiness and joy,

Divine Mercy, in calling us forth from nothingness
to existence,

Divine Mercy, embracing all the works of his hands,

Divine Mercy, crown of all of God's handiwork,

Divine Mercy, in which we are all immersed,

Divine Mercy, sweet relief for anguished hearts,

Divine Mercy, only hope of despairing souls,

Divine Mercy, repose of hearts, peace amidst fear,

Divine Mercy, delight and ecstasy of holy souls,

Divine Mercy, inspiring hope against all hope.

Let us pray:

Eternal God, in whom mercy is endless and the treasury of compassion inexhaustible, look kindly upon us and increase your mercy in us, that in difficult moments we might not despair nor become despondent, but with great confidence submit ourselves to your holy will, which is Love and Mercy itself. Amen.

PRAYERS TO OUR LADY

The Holy Rosary

The Holy Rosary is composed of twenty "decades", each comprising the Our Father, ten Hail Marys, and the Glory be, recited in honour of some mystery in the life of Our Lord or his Blessed Mother. We pray to practise the virtue specially taught by that mystery.

I. The Five Joyful Mysteries
(Mondays, Saturdays)

1. The Annunciation. (*Luke* 1:26-38)

2. The Visitation. (*Luke* 1:39-45)

3. The Nativity. (*Luke* 2:1-7)

4. The Presentation in the Temple. (*Luke* 2:22-35)

5. The Finding of the Child Jesus in the Temple. (*Luke* 2:41-52)

II. The Five Mysteries of Light
(Thursdays)

1. The Baptism of the Lord. (*Matthew* 3:13-17)

2. The Marriage at Cana. (*John* 2:1-12)

3. The Proclamation of the Kingdom and call to conversion. (*Mark* 1:14-15; 2:3-12)

4. The Transfiguration. (*Luke* 9:28-36)

5. The Institution of the Eucharist. (*Matthew* 26:26-29)

III. The Five Sorrowful Mysteries
(Tuesdays, Fridays)

1. The Prayer and Agony in the Garden.
   (*Mark* 14:32-42)

2. The Scourging at the Pillar. (*Matthew* 27:15-26)

3. The Crowning with Thorns. (*Matthew* 27:27-31)

4. The Carrying of the Cross.
   (*John* 19:15-17; *Luke* 23:27-32)

5. The Crucifixion and Death. (*Luke* 23:33-38, 44-46)

IV. The Five Glorious Mysteries
(Wednesdays, Sundays)

1. The Resurrection. (*Matthew* 28:1-8)

2. The Ascension of Christ into Heaven. (*Acts* 1:6-11)

3. The Descent of the Holy Spirit. (*Acts* 2:1-12)

4. The Assumption. (*1 Thessalonians* 4:13-18)

5. The Coronation of the Blessed Virgin Mary.
   (*Revelation* 12:1; 14:1-5: *Isaiah* 6:1-3)

The Hail Holy Queen

Hail, holy Queen, mother of mercy;
hail, our life, our sweetness, and our hope!
To you do we cry, poor banished children of Eve; to you
do we send up our sighs,
mourning and weeping in this vale of tears.
Turn then, most gracious advocate,
your eyes of mercy towards us;
and after this our exile,
show unto us the blessed fruit of your womb, Jesus.
O clement, O loving, O sweet Virgin Mary.

> *V.*   Pray for us, O holy Mother of God.

> *R.*   That we may be made worthy of the promises
> of Christ.

Let us pray:

O God, whose only-begotten Son, by his life,
death and Resurrection,

has purchased for us the rewards of eternal life;
grant, we beseech you,
that meditating on these Mysteries of the most holy
Rosary of the Blessed Virgin Mary,
we may both imitate what they contain,
and obtain what they promise,
through the same Christ our Lord.
R. Amen.

Litany of the Blessed Virgin Mary

Lord have mercy.
Lord have mercy.
Christ have mercy.
Christ have mercy.
Lord have mercy.
Lord have mercy.
Christ hear us.
Christ graciously hear us.

God the Father of heaven, *have mercy on us. (repeat)*
God the Son, Redeemer of the world,
God the Holy Spirit,
Holy Trinity, one God,

Holy Mary, *pray for us. (repeat)*
Holy Mother of God,
Holy Virgin of virgins,
Mother of Christ,
Mother of the Church,
Mother of divine grace,
Mother most pure,
Mother most chaste,
Mother inviolate,
Mother undefiled,
Mother most lovable,
Mother most admirable,
Mother of good counsel,
Mother of our Creator,
Mother of our Saviour,
Virgin most prudent,
Virgin most venerable,
Virgin most renowned,
Virgin most powerful,

Virgin most merciful, *pray for us. (repeat)*
Virgin most faithful,
Mirror of justice,
Seat of wisdom,
Cause of our joy,
Spiritual vessel,
Vessel of honour,
Singular vessel of devotion,
Mystical rose,
Tower of David,
Tower of ivory,
House of gold,
Ark of the Covenant,
Gate of heaven,
Morning Star,
Health of the sick,
Refuge of sinners,
Comfort of the afflicted,
Help of Christians,
Queen of Angels,
Queen of Patriarchs,
Queen of Prophets,
Queen of Apostles
Queen of Martyrs,
Queen of Confessors,
Queen of Virgins,
Queen of all Saints,
Queen conceived without original sin,
Queen assumed into heaven,
Queen of the most holy Rosary,
Queen of the Family,
Queen of Peace.

Lamb of God, you take away the sins of the world,
spare us, O Lord.

Lamb of God, you take away the sins of the world,
graciously hear us, O Lord.

Lamb of God, you take away the sins of the world,
have mercy on us.

The Memorare

Remember, O most loving Virgin Mary,
that it is a thing unheard of,
that anyone ever had recourse to your protection,
implored your help,
or sought your intercession,
and was left forsaken.
Filled therefore with confidence in your goodness
    I fly to you,
O Mother, Virgin of virgins.
To you I come, before you I stand, a sorrowful sinner.
Despise not my poor words,
O Mother of the Word of God,
but graciously hear and grant my prayer.
Amen.

The Regina Caeli

V.   O Queen of heaven, rejoice! Alleluia.

R.   For he whom you did merit to bear, Alleluia,

V.   Has risen as he said, Alleluia.

R.   Pray for us to God, Alleluia.

V.   Rejoice and be glad, O Virgin Mary, Alleluia,

R.   For the Lord has risen indeed, Alleluia.

Let us pray:

God our Father, you give joy to the world
by the Resurrection of your Son,
our Lord Jesus Christ.
Through the prayers of his Mother, the Virgin Mary,
bring us to the happiness of eternal life.
We ask this through our Lord Jesus Christ, your Son,
who lives and reigns with you and the Holy Spirit,
one God, for ever and ever.

R. Amen.

The Holy Family of Jesus, Mary and Joseph

This feast commemorates the unity and love of Jesus, Mary his mother and Joseph, his foster father, as lived out in Bethlehem, Egypt, and Nazareth, and promotes the life they lived as the ideal of family life which all Christian families should seek to emulate.

It is celebrated on the Sunday within the Octave of the Nativity of the Lord, or, if there is no Sunday, on 30 December.

Collect from the Missal

O God, who were pleased to give us the shining example of the Holy Family,
graciously grant that we may imitate them in
practising the virtues of family life
and in the bonds of charity,
and so, in the joy of your house,
delight one day in eternal rewards.
Through our Lord Jesus Christ, your Son,
who lives and reigns with you
in the unity of the Holy Spirit,
one God, for ever and ever.

Concluding Prayer from the Liturgy of the Hours

God our Father, in the Holy Family of Nazareth
you have given us the true model
of a Christian home.
Grant that by following Jesus,
Mary and Joseph in their love for each other
and in the example of their family life
we may come to your home of peace and joy.

1 January - Solemnity of Mary, the Holy Mother of God

This feast of the Blessed Virgin Mary, the Theotokos, or Mother of God, is held on the first day of the New Year, the Octave day of Christmas. It celebrates Mary's motherhood of Jesus, and the term Theotokos or God-bearer was adopted by the First Council of Ephesus (431), in order to safeguard the Divinity and humanity of Christ.

Collect from the Missal

O God, who through the fruitful virginity
of Blessed Mary bestowed on the human race
the grace of eternal salvation,
grant, we pray, that we may experience
the intercession of her,
through whom we were found worthy
to receive the author of life,
our Lord Jesus Christ, your Son.
Who lives and reigns with you
in the unity of the Holy Spirit,
one God, for ever and ever.

2 February - the Presentation of the Lord

The Presentation of the Lord, popularly known as "Candlemas", traditionally concludes the celebration of the season of Christmas. It commemorates the presentation of Jesus in the Temple by Our Lady and St Joseph, forty days after his birth, an occasion when offerings were made and the mother was ritually purified.

Collect from the Missal

Almighty ever-living God,
we humbly implore your majesty that,
just as your Only Begotten Son
was presented on this day in the Temple
in the substance of our flesh, so, by your grace, we may
be presented to you with minds made pure.
Through our Lord Jesus Christ, your Son,
who lives and reigns with you
in the unity of the Holy Spirit,
one God, for ever and ever.

11 February - Our Lady of Lourdes

The feast marks the first apparition of the Blessed Virgin Mary in 1858 to fourteen-year-old St Bernadette Soubirous. There were eighteen apparitions in all, the last of which was on 16 July 1858. The message of Lourdes is a call to personal conversion, prayer and charity. In a special way, the shrine has become closely associated with the sick.

Collect from the Missal

Grant us, O merciful God,
protection in our weakness, that we,
who keep the Memorial of the Immaculate Mother of
God, may, with the help of her intercession, rise up
from our iniquities.
Through our Lord Jesus Christ, your Son,
who lives and reigns with you
in the unity of the Holy Spirit,
one God, for ever and ever.

Concluding prayer from the Liturgy of the Hours

Lord of mercy, as we keep the memory of Mary,
the immaculate Mother of God,
who appeared to Bernadette at Lourdes:
grant us through her prayer strength
in our weakness and grace to rise up from our sins.
(*We make our prayer*) through our Lord.

19 March - Solemnity of St Joseph, Spouse of the Blessed Virgin Mary

Although no words of St Joseph are recorded in Sacred Scripture, he has come to be regarded as one of the greatest and most popular saints, largely because of his humility and his closeness to Our Lord. He died before the beginning of Jesus's public ministry and, since he probably died in the presence of Jesus and Mary, is venerated as the patron of a good death. Blessed Pius IX named him patron of the universal church and St John XXIII added his name to the Roman Canon of the Mass. Pope Francis recently added his name to the other Eucharistic Prayers.

Concluding prayer from the Liturgy of the Hours

Almighty God, at the beginnings of our salvation,
when Mary conceived your Son
and brought him forth into the world,
you placed them under Joseph's watchful care.
May his prayer still help your Church
to be an equally faithful guardian of your mysteries
and a sign of Christ to mankind.
Through Christ our Lord.
Amen.

25 March - Solemnity of the Annunciation of the Lord

On the floor of the Holy House in Nazareth, an inscription reads "Verbum caro hic factum est"; "the Word was made flesh here". When the Blessed Virgin said "yes" to the Angel Gabriel, the Word became flesh; the child conceived on this day was born nine months later on Christmas Day to die for our sins and conquer death.

Concluding prayer from the Liturgy of the Hours

Shape us in the likeness of the divine nature
of our Redeemer, whom we believe to be true God
and true man, since it was your will,
Lord God, that he, your Word,
should take to himself our human nature
in the womb of the Blessed Virgin Mary.
(*We make our prayer*) through our Lord.

13 May - Our Lady of Fatima

The Blessed Virgin Mary appeared to three shepherd children at Fatima (Portugal) on the thirteenth day for six consecutive months in 1917. She brought a message of peace and reparation for sin, encouraging devotion to her Immaculate Heart, the recitation of the Holy Rosary, and the Five First Saturdays devotion of reparation.

Collect from the Missal

O God, who chose the Mother of your Son
to be our Mother also, grant us that,
persevering in penance and prayer
for the salvation of the world,
we may further more effectively each day
the reign of Christ.
Who lives and reigns with you
in the unity of the Holy Spirit,
one God, for ever and ever.

31 May - the Visitation of the Blessed Virgin Mary

The Visitation commemorates the meeting between Mary and her cousin St Elizabeth at Ein Kerem, just outside Jerusalem. Feeling the presence of his Divine Saviour, St John the Baptist leapt in his mother's womb on the Blessed Virgin's arrival. Following St Elizabeth's words of greeting, Our Lady proclaimed the Magnificat, a hymn praising the Lord for all that he had done for his handmaid and expressing her attitude of faith and humility.

Collect from the Missal

Almighty ever-living God, who,
while the Blessed Virgin Mary was carrying
your Son in her womb,
inspired her to visit Elizabeth, grant us, we pray, that,
faithful to the promptings of the Spirit,
we may magnify your greatness
with the Virgin Mary at all times.
Through our Lord Jesus Christ, your Son,
who lives and reigns with you
in the unity of the Holy Spirit,
one God, for ever and ever.

The Immaculate Heart
of the Blessed Virgin Mary

(Saturday following the Second Sunday after Pentecost)

Devotion to the Immaculate Heart of Mary originated with St John Eudes in the seventeenth century and developed in parallel to devotion to the Sacred Heart of Jesus. Whereas the Sacred Heart shows the infinite love of God for mankind, Mary's Immaculate Heart presents us with a model for how we should love God. Honouring her Immaculate Heart not only rightly acknowledges her unique privileges but also leads us to her Son.

Collect from the Missal

O God, who prepared a fit dwelling place
for the Holy Spirit in the Heart
of the Blessed Virgin Mary,
graciously grant that through her intercession
we may be a worthy temple of your glory.
Through our Lord Jesus Christ, your Son,
who lives and reigns with you
in the unity of the Holy Spirit,
one God, for ever and ever.

16 July - Our Lady of Mount Carmel

This feast honours the Blessed Virgin as patroness of the Carmelite Order, which originated on Mt Carmel in Israel. It later came to be associated with a vision of St Simon Stock, said to have taken place on 16 July 1251. Wearing the "Brown Scapular", a symbol of the Carmelite habit, is a sign of trust in Mary's maternal help, especially at the hour of death.

Collect from the Missal

May the venerable intercession of the glorious Virgin Mary come to our aid, we pray, O Lord,
so that, fortified by her protection,
we may reach the mountain which is Christ.
Who lives and reigns with you
in the unity of the Holy Spirit,
one God, for ever and ever.

26 July - Saints Joachim and Anne, Parents of the Blessed Virgin Mary

Saints Joachim and Anne were the parents of the Blessed Virgin Mary and the grandparents of the Lord. They remind us that the Word truly became flesh in a particular family. Our devotion to them is an extension of our love of Mary and her Divine Son.

Collect from the Missal

O Lord, God of our Fathers,
who bestowed on Saints Joachim
and Anne this grace,
that of them should be born the Mother
of your incarnate Son, grant,
through the prayers of both,
that we may attain the salvation you have promised
    to your people.
Through our Lord Jesus Christ, your Son,
who lives and reigns with you
in the unity of the Holy Spirit,
one God, for ever and ever.

5 August - the Dedication of the Basilica of St Mary Major

In the early fifth century, Pope Sixtus III dedicated the restored Basilica of St Mary Major in Rome to Mary, Mother of God. According to tradition its location had originally been indicated by a miraculous shower of snow on 5 August, in the middle of the Roman summer, hence the title "Our Lady of the Snows". The basilica is considered the most important church dedicated to the Blessed Virgin Mary and the festival of its dedication renews our links with Rome.

Collect from the Missal

Pardon the faults of your servants, we pray, O Lord,
that we, who cannot please you by our own deeds,
may be saved through the intercession
of the Mother of your Son and our Lord.
Who lives and reigns with you
in the unity of the Holy Spirit,
one God, for ever and ever.

15 August - the Assumption of the Blessed Virgin Mary

The Solemnity of the Assumption is, in some ways, the paramount feast of Our Lady, since it commemorates her passing, body and soul, into glory in heaven, where she stands beside her Son "in garments of gold". The dogma of the Assumption was only defined in 1950, but it was widely believed by the earliest Christians. The Blessed Virgin truly leads the way; she fulfilled her vocation in humility and, given her Immaculate Conception, the grave was no place for her body. Where she is now, we one day hope to be.

Vigil Mass

Collect from the Missal

O God, who, looking on the lowliness of the Blessed Virgin Mary, raised her to this grace,
that your Only Begotten Son was born of her
according to the flesh and that she was crowned this
    day with surpassing glory,
grant through her prayers, that,
saved by the mystery of your redemption,
we may merit to be exalted by you on high.
Through our Lord Jesus Christ, your Son,
who lives and reigns with you
in the unity of the Holy Spirit,
one God, for ever and ever.

Mass during the Day

Collect from the Missal

Almighty ever-living God,
who assumed the Immaculate Virgin Mary,
the Mother of your Son,
body and soul into heavenly glory, grant, we pray, that,
always attentive to the things that are above,
we may merit to be sharers of her glory.
Through our Lord Jesus Christ, your Son,
who lives and reigns with you
in the unity of the Holy Spirit,
one God, for ever and ever.

Concluding Prayer from the Liturgy of the Hours

Almighty, ever-living God,
you have taken the mother of your Son,
the immaculate Virgin Mary,
body and soul into the glory where you dwell.
Keep our hearts set on heaven so that, with her,
we may share in your glory.
(*We make our prayer*) through our Lord.

17 August - Our Lady of Knock

In August 1879, fifteen people witnessed an apparition of Our Lady, St Joseph and St John the Evangelist, together with the Lord (as the Lamb of God), outside the church at Knock, in Ireland. It grew into an international shrine and was visited by St John Paul II in 1979.

Collect from the Missal

O God, who give hope to your people
in time of distress,
grant that we who keep the memorial
of the Blessed Virgin, Our Lady of Knock, may, through
her intercession, be steadfast in the faith
during our earthly pilgrimage to heaven,
and so come to eternal glory
with all the Angels and the Saints.
Through our Lord Jesus Christ, your Son,
who lives and reigns with you
in the unity of the Holy Spirit,
one God, for ever and ever.

22 August - the Queenship of the Blessed Virgin Mary

Pope Pius XII instituted this feast in 1954, to conclude what was then the Octave of the Assumption. We remember that the Blessed Virgin reigns in heaven, together with her Son; she reigns not because she is equal to God but because she is mother of Christ the King. All her privileges come from her Motherhood of God and the unique role she played in our redemption.

Collect from the Missal

O God, who made the Mother of your Son
to be our Mother and our Queen,
graciously grant that,
sustained by her intercession,
we may attain in the heavenly Kingdom
the glory promised to your children.
Through our Lord Jesus Christ, your Son,
who lives and reigns with you
in the unity of the Holy Spirit,
one God, for ever and ever.

8 September - the Nativity of the Blessed Virgin Mary

Nothing is known for sure about the details of the Blessed Virgin's birth, and her parents, traditionally known as St Joachim and St Anne, are not mentioned in Sacred Scripture. Today's feast originated in the East, probably during the sixth century, and was later introduced to the West. Her earthly birth is celebrated (like that of St John the Baptist) because it announced to the world the coming of Jesus, the beginning of the New Covenant.

Collect from the Missal

Impart to your servants, we pray, O Lord,
the gift of heavenly grace,
that the Feast of the Nativity
    of the Blessed Virgin may bring deeper peace
to those for whom the birth of her Son
was the dawning of salvation.
Through our Lord Jesus Christ, your Son,
who lives and reigns with you
in the unity of the Holy Spirit,
one God, for ever and ever.

12 September - the Most Holy Name of Mary

The name of Mary is regarded as holy because it is the name of the Mother of God, her who brought the Saviour into the world. The Feast of the Most Holy Name of Mary was added to the Universal Calendar in 1684 by Blessed Innocent XI, commemorating the defeat of the Turks at the gates of Vienna the previous year: a powerful example of the might of the Blessed Virgin's intercession.

Collect from the Missal

Grant, we pray, almighty God, that,
for all who celebrate the glorious Name
of the Blessed Virgin Mary,
she may obtain your merciful favour.
Through our Lord Jesus Christ, your Son,
who lives and reigns with you
in the unity of the Holy Spirit,
one God, for ever and ever.

15 September - Our Lady of Sorrows

This feast originated as a memorial of the Seven Sorrows of Mary, most of which were linked to the events of Good Friday, when she stood at the foot of the Cross. We remember that the Blessed Virgin had to live through the personal tragedy of seeing her Son die. She had a unique share in our redemption, offering her Son's life to the Lord, trusting that it was part of his plan.

Collect from the Missal

O God, who willed that,
when your Son was lifted high on the Cross,
his Mother should stand close by
and share his suffering, grant that your Church,
participating with the Virgin Mary
in the Passion of Christ,
may merit a share in his Resurrection.
Who lives and reigns with you
in the unity of the Holy Spirit,
one God, for ever and ever.

24 September - Our Lady of Walsingham

England's premier Marian shrine dates back to 1061, when a wealthy widow, Richeldis de Faverches, was inspired by a vision to build a replica of the Holy House of Nazareth in Walsingham, Norfolk. This remained a vibrant pilgrimage centre until its destruction in 1538, although the shrine was later revived by both Catholics (1897) and Anglicans (1922). Formerly, 24 September was kept as the Memorial of Our Lady of Ransom, when prayers were offered for the "ransom" of England, "Our Lady's Dowry".

Collect from the Missal

Grant, we pray, almighty God,
that as in the mystery of the Incarnation
the Blessed and ever Virgin Mary
conceived your Son in her heart before she
conceived him in the womb, so we,
your pilgrim people, rejoicing in her motherly care,
may welcome him into our hearts
and become a holy house fit for his eternal dwelling.
Who lives and reigns with you
in the unity of the Holy Spirit,
one God, for ever and ever.

7 October - Our Lady of the Rosary

This Memorial (originally Our Lady of Victories) commemorates the battle of Lepanto (7 October 1571), when a Christian fleet defeated the Turks. The victory was attributed by Pope St Pius V to the recitation of the Holy Rosary. This great Marian prayer is traced back to St Dominic and his confrères, preaching against the Albigensian heresy in the thirteenth century, but it reached its familiar form in the fifteenth century. Since then it has spread all over the world and has produced marvellous fruits, bringing countless Christians "to Jesus through Mary."

Collect from the Missal

Pour forth, we beseech you, O Lord,
  your grace into our hearts,
that we, to whom the Incarnation
of Christ your Son
was made known by the message of an Angel,
may, through the intercession
of the Blessed Virgin Mary,
by his Passion and Cross
be brought to the glory of his Resurrection.
Who lives and reigns with you
in the unity of the Holy Spirit,
one God, for ever and ever.

21 November - The Presentation of the Blessed Virgin Mary

The Presentation of Mary in the Temple as a young girl is based not on the New Testament but on an account in the apocryphal Protoevangelium of James. In doing this, the Blessed Virgin dedicated herself to the service of God and was thus open to God's will. The feast prepares us for Advent and Christmas, when we celebrate the coming of her Divine Son into the world.

Collect from the Missal

As we venerate the glorious memory
of the most holy Virgin Mary,
grant, we pray, O Lord, through her intercession, that
we, too, may merit to receive
from the fullness of your grace.
Through our Lord Jesus Christ, your Son,
who lives and reigns with you
in the unity of the Holy Spirit,
one God, for ever and ever.

8 December - Solemnity of the Immaculate Conception of the Blessed Virgin Mary

This Solemnity celebrates the Blessed Virgin's unique privilege of being preserved from the stain of sin at the very moment of her conception. This was fitting for she would one day carry the second person of the Trinity in her womb. But with Mary, the manner in which she was saved was exceptional: from the first moment of her existence, she was free from the stain of original sin. This dogma was solemnly defined by Blessed Pius IX on 8 December 1854 but had long been widely believed by Christians.

Collect from the Missal

O God, who by the Immaculate Conception of the Blessed Virgin prepared

a worthy dwelling for your Son, grant,
we pray, that, as you preserved her from every stain
by virtue of the Death of your Son, which you foresaw,
so, through her intercession, we, too,
may be cleansed and admitted to your presence.
Through our Lord Jesus Christ, your Son,
who lives and reigns with you
in the unity of the Holy Spirit,
one God, for ever and ever.

12 December - Our Lady of Guadalupe

On 9 December 1531, the Blessed Virgin Mary appeared to St Juan Diego and left an image of herself imprinted upon his cloak. The image was placed in a magnificent shrine where it became an object of great devotion and encouraged the conversion of the Mexican people to Christ. Many miracles were attributed to her intercession and Our Lady of Guadalupe was named as "Queen of Mexico and Empress of the Americas".

Collect from the Missal

O God, Father of mercies,
who placed your people under the singular
protection of your Son's most holy Mother,
grant that all who invoke the Blessed Virgin
of Guadalupe, may seek with ever more lively faith
the progress of peoples in the ways of justice
and of peace.
Through our Lord Jesus Christ, your Son,
who lives and reigns with you
in the unity of the Holy Spirit,
one God, for ever and ever.

25 December - The Nativity of the Lord

Christmas Day

Christmas Day is the culmination of the Advent Season, and the glorious commemoration of the Birth of Our Lord Jesus Christ of the Blessed Virgin Mary. His birth was foretold by the prophets, and long awaited. Our Lady and St Joseph travelled to Bethlehem for a census, and it was here that Jesus was born. But it happened in silence, poverty and humility, and the first people to see the Infant Christ were poor shepherds.

At the Mass during the Day

Collect from the Missal

O God, who wonderfully created the dignity
of human nature and still more wonderfully
restored it, grant, we pray,
that we may share in the divinity of Christ,
who humbled himself to share in our humanity.
Who lives and reigns with you
in the unity of the Holy Spirit,
one God, for ever and ever.

Concluding Prayer from the Liturgy of the Hours

God our Father, our human nature is the wonderful
work of your hands,
made still more wonderful
by your work of redemption.
Your Son took to himself our manhood,
grant us a share in the godhead of Jesus Christ,
who lives and reigns with you and the Holy Spirit,
God for ever and ever.

Prayers From Approved Marian Apparitions

Guadalupe

Our Lady appeared to St Juan Diego at Tepeyac hill, near Mexico city, several times in 1531 and left the miraculous image of Guadalupe imprinted on his cloak.

Pope St Pius X's Prayer to Our Lady of Guadalupe

Our Lady of Guadalupe, Mystical Rose,
make intercession for the holy Church,
protect the Sovereign Pontiff,
help all those who invoke thee in their necessities,
and since thou art the ever Virgin Mary
   and Mother of the true God,
obtain for us from thy most holy Son
   the grace of keeping our faith,
sweet hope in the midst of the bitterness of life,
burning charity and the precious gift
of final perseverance. Amen.

Rue du Bac

Our Lady appeared several times to St Catherine Labouré at the Rue du Bac convent in Paris, France, in 1830, asking her to have struck a medal dedicated to her Immaculate Conception.

Prayer on the Miraculous Medal

O Mary, conceived without sin,
pray for us who have recourse to thee!

Lourdes

Our Lady appeared to St Bernadette Soubirous at Lourdes, France, in 1858, with a message of prayer and penance. She revealed the miraculous spring at the Grotto, which has been a source of healing for many.

Pope St John Paul II - Prayer at the Lourdes Grotto in the Vatican Gardens

O blessed Virgin, Mother of God, Mother of Christ, Mother of the Church,
look upon us mercifully at this hour.
Faithful Virgin, pray for us.
Teach us to believe as you believed.

Make our faith in God, in Christ, in the Church,
always to be serene, courageous, strong, and generous.
Mother worthy of love.
Mother of faithful love, pray for us.
Teach us to love God and our brothers and sisters
    as you loved them: make our love for others
to be always patient, kindly, and respectful.
Cause of our joy, pray for us.
Teach us to be able to grasp, in faith,
the paradox of Christian joy,
which springs up and blooms from sorrow,
renunciation, and union with your sacrificed Son.
Make our joy to be always genuine and full,
in order to be able to communicate it to all.
Amen.

Fatima

Our Lady appeared to the three young seers, St Jacinta and St Francisco Marto, and Lúcia dos Santos at Fatima in Portugal, between May and October of 1917, with a message of prayer and penance. On 13 October 1917, the Blessed Virgin performed the great miracle of the sun, as proof of her apparitions, and that all might believe.

Fatima Prayers

Reparation Prayer of the Angel
- given to the three seers in the Autumn of 1916

O Most Holy Trinity, Father, Son and Holy Spirit, I adore thee profoundly.
I offer thee the most precious Body, Blood, Soul and Divinity of Jesus Christ present
  in all the tabernacles of the world,
in reparation for the outrages,
sacrileges and indifferences by which he is offended.
And by the infinite merits of the Sacred Heart of Jesus and the Immaculate Heart of Mary
I beg the conversion of poor sinners.

Sacrifice Prayer - given to the seers by Our Lady on 13 June 1917, and to be said when making a sacrifice or offering up an action in reparation

O Jesus, it is for your love,
  for the conversion of sinners,
and in reparation for sins committed against
  the Immaculate Heart of Mary.

Litany of Our Lady of Fatima

Our Lady of Fatima, *pray for our dear country.*
Our Lady of Fatima, *sanctify our clergy.*
Our Lady of Fatima,
  make our Catholics more fervent.
Our Lady of Fatima,
  guide and inspire those who govern us.
Our Lady of Fatima, *cure the sick who confide in thee.*
Our Lady of Fatima,
  console the sorrowful who trust in thee.
Our Lady of Fatima, *help those who invoke your aid.*
Our Lady of Fatima, *deliver us from all dangers.*
Our Lady of Fatima, *help us to resist temptation.*
Our Lady of Fatima,
  obtain for us all that we lovingly ask of thee.
Our Lady of Fatima, *help those who are dear to us.*
Our Lady of Fatima,
  bring back to the right road our erring brothers.
Our Lady of Fatima, *give us back our ancient fervour.*

Our Lady of Fatima,
  *obtain for us pardon of our manifold sins
  and offences.*
Our Lady of Fatima,
  bring all men to the feet of thy Divine Child.
Our Lady of Fatima, *obtain peace for the world.*
O Mary conceived without sin,
  pray for us who have recourse to thee.
Immaculate Heart of Mary,
pray for us now and at the hour of our death.
Amen.

Let us Pray:

O God of infinite goodness and mercy,
fill our hearts with a great confidence
in thy dear Mother,
whom we invoke under the title of
Our Lady of the Rosary and Our Lady of Fatima
and grant us by her powerful intercession
all the graces, spiritual and temporal,
which we need. Through Christ our Lord.
Amen.

The Story of Knock

At about eight o'clock on the Thursday evening of 21 August 1879, the Blessed Virgin Mary, St Joseph and St John the Evangelist appeared at the south gable of the church at Knock, County Mayo, Ireland. Beside them and a little to the right was an altar with a cross and the figure of a lamb, around which angels hovered.

Novena to Our Lady of Knock

In the name of the Father,
and of the Son,
and of the Holy Spirit,
Amen.

Give praise to the Father Almighty,
To his Son, Jesus Christ the Lord,
To the Spirit who lives in our hearts,
Both now and forever.
Amen.

Our Lady of Knock, Queen of Ireland,
you gave hope to your people in a time of distress,
and comforted them in sorrow.
You have inspired countless pilgrims to pray with
confidence to your divine Son,
remembering his promise,
"Ask and you shall receive, seek and you shall find."
Help me to remember that we are all pilgrims
    on the road to heaven.
Fill me with love and concern
    for my brothers and sisters in Christ,
especially those who live with me.
Comfort me when I am sick, lonely or depressed.
Teach me how to take part ever more reverently
    in the Holy Mass.
Give me a greater love of Jesus
    in the Blessed Sacrament.
Pray for me now, and at the hour of my death. Amen.

Lamb of God, you take away the sins of the world;
Have mercy on us.

Lamb of God, you take away the sins of the world;
Have mercy on us.

Lamb of God, you take away the sins of the world;
Grant us peace.

St Joseph

Chosen by God to be
the Husband of Mary,
the Protector of the Holy Family,
the Guardian of the Church.
Protect all families
In their work and recreation
And guard us on our journey through life.

(Repeat Lamb of God… *as above)*

St John

Beloved Disciple of the Lord,
Faithful priest.
Teacher of the Word of God.
Help us to hunger for the Word.
To be loyal to the Mass
And to love one another.

(Repeat Lamb of God… *on previous page)*

Our Lady of Knock *Pray for us. (repeat)*
Refuge of sinners
Queen Assumed into Heaven
Queen of the Rosary
Mother of Nazareth
Queen of Virgins
Help of Christians
Health of the Sick
Queen of Peace
Our Lady, Queen and Mother
Our Lady, Mother of the Church

(Here mention your own special intentions)

With the Angels and Saints let us pray:
give praise to the Father Almighty,
to his Son, Jesus Christ the Lord,
to the Spirit who lives in our hearts,
both now and forever.
Amen.

Instruction - The Rosary or Mass and Holy Communion is recommended each day.

Mary in the Bible

The following Biblical passages relate to Our Lady. Those from the Old Testament indicate that Mary can be seen as being prefigured, in the prophetic sense, as the mother of the Redeemer and Messiah, while those from the New Testament show how her life with Christ unfolded.

Old Testament passages

Genesis 3:9-15 - the Protoevangelium
- the Promise of the Redeemer

After the Fall of Adam and Eve, God punished the devil and promised that the offspring of the woman, Jesus, the New Adam, son of Mary, the New Eve, would crush the head of Satan. This is the Protoevangelium, the "first Gospel", the promise of the Redeemer to come in the fullness of time.

Genesis 28:12-15 - Jacob's Ladder as a type of Mary

Just as Jacob saw in a vision a ladder extending from earth to heaven, so is Mary the ladder by which Jesus descended to earth, taking on human nature, as well as being the way, as the Mediatrix of all graces, by which through her intercession we receive grace.

Exodus 3:1-4 - The Burning Bush as a type of Mary

Just as Moses saw the bush burning, but it was not consumed, so Mary's virginity remained whole before, during and after Christ's birth, as she became a mother in a miraculous way.

Exodus 40:20 - the Ark of the Covenant as a type of Mary

Just as the Ark contained the tablets of the Mosaic Law, so Mary bore the heir to this Law, Jesus Christ, and just as the Ark was covered inside and out with gold, so Mary, the new Ark of the Covenant, shone with the golden brilliance of a matchless purity.

Numbers 17 - Aaron's rod as a type of Mary

Just as Aaron's rod sprouted miraculously, giving forth buds, blossoms and fruit, so Mary brought forth Christ without loss of her virginity and free from pain, as the temple of the Holy Spirit.

Judges 6:36-40 - Gideon's Fleece as a type of Mary

Just as Gideon's fleece was wet while the ground was dry around it on the first morning, while it was dry and the ground wet the next day, so firstly the Son of God descended from heaven into her womb, and secondly, Mary was full of grace from her conception while the rest of humanity was affected by original sin.

Isaiah 7:14-16 - the prophetic sign of the Virgin Birth

Isaiah gave King Ahaz the sign of the Virgin Birth of the Son who would be called Emmanuel, that is, "God with us", in other words the Incarnation of Christ at Bethlehem, through the miracle of the Virgin Birth.

Ezekiel 44:2 - Mary as the Eastern Gate of the Temple

Just as the Eastern Gate of the Temple, according to Ezekiel, would remain shut because the Lord, the God of Israel, had passed through it, so Mary was the closed Gate who retained her virginity after the birth of Christ.

Micah 5:2-3 - the Ruler of Israel, the Messiah, is to come from Bethlehem

Jesus was born in Bethlehem to Mary, as the prophet Micah had foretold: his origin was from of old, from ancient days, because he was the incarnate Son of God.

New Testament passages

Luke 1:26-38 - the Annunciation of the Angel Gabriel to Mary, who told her that she was to be the Mother of God.

Mary's yes to God led to the Incarnation of Jesus in her womb.

Luke 1:39-45 - The Magnificat

This passage deals with the Visitation of Mary to her cousin Elizabeth, who was carrying St John the Baptist, and was the occasion of her hymn of praise, the Magnificat.

Matthew 1:18-24 - the Birth of Our Lord to Our Lady

St Matthew's account focuses on how an Angel of the Lord appeared to St Joseph in a dream to reassure him that Mary had remained faithful and that she had conceived her child by the power of the Holy Spirit.

Luke 2:1-14 - the Birth of Our Lord

After Mary and Joseph had gone to Bethlehem for Caesar Augustus's census, Jesus was born there in humility and poverty, because there was no place for them at the inn.

Luke 2:15-20 - the Shepherds go to see the Holy Family

After they had been told of Christ's birth by a vision of angels, the shepherds visited the Holy Family in their shelter at Bethlehem.

Luke 2:22-40 - the Presentation of the Child Jesus in the Temple forty days after his birth by Mary and Joseph.

When the aged Simeon saw the Child, he foretold that a sword of sorrow would pierce the Blessed Virgin's heart at the time of the crucifixion.

Matthew 2:1-12 - the Visit of the Wise Men to see the Child Jesus.

After King Herod had tried to deceive the Magi they visited the Holy Family at Bethlehem, but returned by a different way to their own country. This is the Epiphany, or manifestation of Christ to the Gentiles.

Luke 2:41-51 - the finding of the Child Jesus in the Temple by Mary and Joseph.

After he had been missing for three days, his parents found him, but did not understand when he told them that he had been about his Father's affairs.

John 2:1-11 - The Wedding Feast at Cana.

The Wedding Feast at Cana saw the public manifestation of Jesus as the Messiah, as he turned the water into wine for the guests at the behest of his mother, Mary, thus anticipating his "hour" when his mission as the Redeemer of all mankind would begin.

John 19:25-27 - Mary at the foot of the Cross

This passage describes Mary at the foot of the Cross of her Son, Jesus. He gave John to her as her son, and confided John to Mary as his mother, an indication of how all Christians, who are brothers of Christ, are also Mary's spiritual children.

Acts of the Apostles 1:12-14; 2:1-4 - The decent of the Holy Spirit at Pentecost

Mary, as the Spouse of the Holy Spirit was at the descent of the same Holy Spirit at Pentecost, when the disciples were filled with his power and were able to boldly proclaim the Faith.

Revelation 11:19; 12:1-6,10 - The Assumption

Mary is the Woman of the Apocalypse, the new ark of the covenant, now assumed into heaven, the Woman clothed with the sun, who also has the moon under her feet, symbols of her power as Mother and intercessor for all mankind.

PRAYERS FOR VARIOUS NEEDS & OCCASIONS

Commendation

Jesus, Mary and Joseph,
I give you my heart and my soul.
Jesus, Mary and Joseph,
assist me in my last agony.
Jesus, Mary and Joseph,
may I breathe forth my soul in peace with you.

Act of Resignation

O Lord, my God,
whatever manner of death is pleasing to you,
with all its anguish, pains and sorrows,
I now accept from your hand with a resigned
    and willing spirit.

Prayer of St Ignatius

Teach us, good Lord, to serve you as you deserve;
to give and not to count the cost;
to fight and not to heed the wounds;
to toil and not to seek for rest;
to labour and not to ask for any reward,
save that of knowing that we do your will.
Amen.

Prayer to my guardian angel

O angel of God, my guardian dear
to whom God's love commits me here.
Ever this day/night be at my side
to light, to guard, to rule and guide.
Amen.

Prayer to St Michael

St Michael, the Archangel,
defend us in the day of battle;
be our safeguard against the wickedness
    and snares of the devil.
May God rebuke him, we humbly pray and do you,
O Prince of the heavenly host, by the power of God,
cast into hell Satan and all the other evil spirits
who prowl through the world seeking the ruin of souls.
Amen.

In Temptation

Lord, save me, or I perish.
Keep me close to you by your grace,
or I shall sin and fall away from you.
Jesus, help me;
Mary, help me;
my holy Angel,
watch over me.

In Trouble

In all things may the most holy, the most just,
and the most lovable will of God be done,
praised, and exalted above all for ever.
Your will be done, O Lord, your will be done.
The Lord has given, the Lord has taken away;
blessed be the name of the Lord.

In Sickness and Pain

Lord, your will be done; I take this for my sins.
I offer up to you my sufferings,
together with all that my Saviour has suffered
for me; and I beg you, through his sufferings,
to have mercy on me.
Free me from this illness and pain if you will,
and if it be for my good.
You love me too much to let me suffer
   unless it be for my good.
Therefore, O Lord, I trust myself to you;
do with me as you please.
In sickness and in health,
I wish to love you always.

Prayer for Chastity

O my God, teach me to love others with the purity
of your holy Mother.
Give me the grace to resist firmly every
temptation to impure thoughts, words or actions.
Teach me always to love with generosity and goodness,
to respect myself and others in the way I act
   and to reverence the way that you have given us
   for the creation of new life.

In Thanksgiving

My God, from my heart I thank you for the many blessings you have given to me.
I thank you for having created and baptised me, and for having placed me in your holy Catholic Church; and for having given me so many graces and mercies
   through the merits of Jesus Christ.
And I thank you, dear Jesus,
for having become a little child for my sake,
to teach me to be holy and humble like you;
and for having died upon the Cross
that I might have pardon for my sins and get to heaven.
Also I thank you for all your other mercies,
most of all for those you have given me today.

Prayer for the Pope

O almighty and eternal God,
have mercy on your servant our Holy Father,
the Pope, and direct him according to your
clemency into the way of everlasting salvation;
that he may desire by your grace those things
   that are agreeable to you,
and perform them with all his strength.
Through Christ our Lord. Amen.

Prayer for Priests

Father, you have appointed your Son
Jesus Christ eternal High Priest.
Guide those he has chosen to be ministers of word
   and sacrament and help them to be faithful
   in fulfilling the ministry they have received.
Grant this through our Lord Jesus Christ, your Son,
who lives and reigns with you and the Holy Spirit,
one God, for ever and ever. Amen.

Prayer for Vocations

Lord Jesus Christ, Shepherd of souls,
who called the Apostles to be fishers of men,
raise up new apostles in your holy Church.
Teach them that to serve you is to reign:
to possess you is to possess all things.
Kindle in the young hearts of our sons and daughters
the fire of zeal for souls.
Make them eager to spread your kingdom on earth.
Grant them courage to follow you, who are the Way,
the Truth and the Life;
who live and reign for ever and ever.
Amen.

Mary, Queen of the Clergy, pray for us.
Help our students who are preparing
for the priesthood.

Prayer for Others

O Jesus, have mercy on your holy Church;
take care of her.

O Jesus, have pity on poor sinners,
and save them from hell.

O Jesus, bless my father, my mother,
my brothers and sisters,
and all I ought to pray for,
as your Heart knows how to bless them.

O Jesus, have pity on the poor souls in purgatory
and give them eternal rest.

Prayer for Christian Unity

Look mercifully, Lord, on your people,
and pour out on us the gifts of your Holy Spirit.
Grant that we may constantly grow
    in love of the truth,
and seek the perfect unity of Christians
    in our prayers and our deeds.
Through Christ our Lord. Amen.

Prayer for Peace

O God, from whom are holy desires,
right counsels and just deeds,
give to your servants that peace which
    the world cannot give;
that we may serve you with our whole hearts,
and live quiet lives under your protection,
free from the fear of our enemies.
Through Christ our Lord. Amen.

Anima Christi

Soul of Christ, sanctify me.
Body of Christ, save me.
Blood of Christ, inebriate me.
Water from the side of Christ, wash me.
Passion of Christ, strengthen me.
O good Jesus, hear me.
Within thy wounds hide me.
Suffer me not to be separated from thee.
From the malicious enemy defend me.
In the hour of my death call me,
And bid me to come to thee.
That with thy saints I may praise thee,
For all eternity. Amen.

THE ORDER
OF MASS

Introductory Rites

The faithful dispose themselves properly to celebrate the Eucharist.

Before Mass begins, the people gather in a spirit of recollection, preparing for their participation in the Mass.

All stand during the entrance procession.

Sign of the Cross

After the Entrance Chant, the Priest and the faithful sign themselves with the Sign of the Cross:

Priest: In the name of the Father,
and of the Son,
and of the Holy Spirit.

Response: **Amen.**

Greeting

The Priest greets the people, with one of the following:

1. **Pr.** The grace of our Lord Jesus Christ,
and the love of God,
and the communion of the Holy Spirit
be with you all.

2. **Pr.** Grace to you and peace from God
our Father and the Lord Jesus Christ.

3. **Pr.** The Lord be with you.

The people reply:

R.   **And with your spirit.**

The Priest, or a Deacon, or another minister, may very briefly introduce the faithful to the Mass of the day.

Penitential Act

There are three forms of the Penitential Act which may be chosen from as appropriate.

Pr. Brethren (brothers and sisters),
let us acknowledge our sins,
and so prepare ourselves to celebrate
the sacred mysteries.

A brief pause for silence follows.

Then one of the following forms is used:

1. **I confess to almighty God**
and to you, my brothers and sisters,
that I have greatly sinned,
in my thoughts and in my words,
in what I have done and in what
   I have failed to do,
   and, striking their breast, they say:
   through my fault, through my fault,
   through my most grievous fault;
   therefore I ask blessed Mary ever-Virgin,
   all the Angels and Saints,
   and you, my brothers and sisters,
   to pray for me to the Lord our God.

2. **Pr.** Have mercy on us, O Lord.
R. **For we have sinned against you.**

Pr. Show us, O Lord, your mercy.
R. **And grant us your salvation.**

Invocations naming the gracious works of the Lord may be made, as in the example below:

3. Pr. You were sent to heal the contrite of heart:
Lord, have mercy.   *Or:* Kyrie, eleison.
R.   **Lord, have mercy.**   *Or:* **Kyrie, eleison.**

Pr.   You came to call sinners:
Christ, have mercy.   *Or:* Christe, eleison.
R.   **Christ, have mercy.**   *Or:* **Christe, eleison.**

Pr.   You are seated at the right hand of the Father
to intercede for us:
Lord, have mercy.   *Or:* Kyrie, eleison.
R.   **Lord, have mercy.**   *Or:* **Kyrie, eleison.**

The absolution by the Priest follows:

Pr.   May almighty God have mercy on us,
forgive us our sins,
and bring us to everlasting life.
R.   **Amen.**

The Kyrie, eleison (Lord, have mercy) invocations follow, unless they have just occurred.

Pr.   Lord, have mercy.   **R. Lord, have mercy.**
Pr.   Christ, have mercy.   **R. Christ, have mercy.**
Pr.   Lord, have mercy.   **R. Lord, have mercy.**

Or:

Pr.   Kyrie, eleison.   **R. Kyrie, eleison.**
Pr.   Christe, eleison.   **R. Christe, eleison.**
Pr.   Kyrie, eleison.   **R. Kyrie, eleison.**

The Gloria

On Sundays (outside of Advent and Lent), Solemnities and Feast Days, this hymn is either sung or said:

Glory to God in the highest,
and on earth peace to people of good will.
We praise you,
we bless you,
we adore you,
we glorify you,
we give you thanks for your great glory,
Lord God, heavenly King,
O God, almighty Father.

Lord Jesus Christ, Only Begotten Son,
Lord God, Lamb of God, Son of the Father,
you take away the sins of the world,
    have mercy on us;
you take away the sins of the world,
    receive our prayer;
you are seated at the right hand of the Father,
have mercy on us.

For you alone are the Holy One,
you alone are the Lord,
you alone are the Most High,
Jesus Christ,
with the Holy Spirit,
in the glory of God the Father.
Amen.

Glória in excélsis Deo
et in terra pax homínibus bonæ voluntátis.
Laudámus te,
benedícimus te,
adorámus te,
glorificámus te,
grátias ágimus tibi propter magnam glóriam tuam.
Dómine Deus, Rex cæléstis,
Deus Pater omnípotens.

Dómine Fili unigénite, Jesu Christe,
Dómine Deus, Agnus Dei, Fílius Patris,
qui tollis peccáta mundi, miserére nobis;
qui tollis peccáta mundi,
    súscipe deprecatiónem nostram.
Qui sedes ad déxteram Patris, miserére nobis.

Quóniam tu solus Sanctus, tu solus Dóminus,
    tu solus Altissimus,
Jesu Christe, cum Sancto Spíritu: in glória Dei Patris.
Amen.

When this hymn is concluded, the Priest says:

Pr.   Let us pray.

And all pray in silence. Then the Priest says the Collect prayer, which ends:

R.   Amen.

The Liturgy of the Word

By hearing the word proclaimed in worship, the faithful again enter into a dialogue with God.

First Reading

The reader goes to the ambo and proclaims the First Reading, while all sit and listen. The reader ends:

The word of the Lord.

R.   **Thanks be to God.**

It is appropriate to have a brief time of quiet between readings as those present take the word of God to heart.

Psalm

The psalmist or cantor sings or says the Psalm, with the people making the response.

Second Reading

On Sundays and certain other days there is a second reading. It concludes with the same response as above.

Gospel

The assembly stands for the Gospel Acclamation. Except during Lent the Acclamation is:

R.   **Alleluia.**

During Lent the following forms are used:

R. **Praise to you, O Christ, King of eternal glory!**
Or:

R. **Praise and honour to you, Lord Jesus!**
Or:

R. **Glory and praise to you, O Christ!**
Or:

R. **Glory to you, O Christ,**
you are the Word of God!

At the ambo the Deacon, or the Priest says:

Pr. The Lord be with you.

R. **And with your spirit.**

Pr. A reading from the holy Gospel according to N.

He makes the Sign of the Cross on the book and, together with the people, on his forehead, lips, and breast.

R. **Glory to you, O Lord.**

At the end of the Gospel:

Pr. The Gospel of the Lord.

R. **Praise to you, Lord Jesus Christ.**

After the Gospel all sit to listen to the Homily.

The Homily

Then follows the Homily, which is preached by a Priest or Deacon on all Sundays and Holydays of Obligation. After a brief silence all stand.

The Creed

On Sundays and Solemnities, the Profession of Faith will follow. The Apostles' Creed may be used.

The Niceno-Constantinopolitan Creed

I believe in one God,
the Father almighty,
maker of heaven and earth,
of all things visible and invisible.

I believe in one Lord Jesus Christ,
the Only Begotten Son of God,
born of the Father before all ages.
God from God, Light from Light,
true God from true God,
begotten, not made, consubstantial with the Father;
through him all things were made.
For us men and for our salvation
he came down from heaven, (*all bow*)
and by the Holy Spirit was incarnate of
    the Virgin Mary, and became man.

For our sake he was crucified under Pontius Pilate,
he suffered death and was buried
and rose again on the third day
in accordance with the Scriptures.
He ascended into heaven
and is seated at the right hand of the Father.
He will come again in glory
to judge the living and the dead
and his kingdom will have no end.

I believe in the Holy Spirit, the Lord, the giver of life,
who proceeds from the Father and the Son,
who with the Father and the Son is adored
    and glorified,
who has spoken through the prophets.

I believe in one, holy, catholic and apostolic Church.
I confess one Baptism for the forgiveness of sins
and I look forward to the resurrection of the dead
and the life of the world to come. Amen.

Credo in unum Deum,
Patrem omnipoténtem,
factórem cæli et terræ,
visibílium ómnium et invisibílium.

Et in unum Dóminum Jesum Christum,
Fílium Dei unigénitum,
et ex Patre natum ante ómnia sáecula.
Deum de Deo, lumen de lúmine,
    Deum verum de Deo vero,
génitum, non factum, consubstantiálem Patri:
per quem ómnia facta sunt.
Qui propter nos hómines et propter nostram salútem
descéndit de cælis. *(all bow)*
Et incarnátus est de Spiritu Sancto
    ex María Vírgine, et homo factus est.

Crucifíxus étiam pro nobis sub Póntio Piláto;
passus et sepúltus est,
et resurréxit tértia die, secúndum Scriptúras,
et ascéndit in cælum, sedet ad déxteram Patris.

Et íterum ventúrus est cum glória,
    iudicáre vivos et mórtuos,
cuius regni non erit finis.
Et in Spiritum Sanctum, Dóminum et vivificántem:
    qui ex Patre Filióque procédit.
Qui cum Patre et Fílio simul adorátur
    et conglorificátur:
qui locútus est per prophétas.

Et unam, sanctam, cathólicam
    et apostólicam Ecclésiam.
Confíteor unum baptísma in remissiónem peccatórum.
Et exspécto resurrectiónem mortuórum,
et vitam ventúri sáeculi.
Amen.

The Apostles' Creed

I believe in God,
the Father almighty,
Creator of heaven and earth,
and in Jesus Christ, his only Son, our Lord,

(all bow)

who was conceived by the Holy Spirit,
born of the Virgin Mary,
suffered under Pontius Pilate,
was crucified, died and was buried;
he descended into hell;
on the third day he rose again from the dead;
he ascended into heaven,
and is seated at the right hand of God
    the Father almighty;
from there he will come to judge the living
    and the dead.

I believe in the Holy Spirit,
the holy catholic Church,
the communion of saints,
the forgiveness of sins,
the resurrection of the body,
and life everlasting.
Amen.

Credo in Deum, Patrem omnipoténtem,
Creatórem caeli et terrae.
Et in Iesum Christum, Fílium eius únicum,
Dóminum nostrum:

(all bow)

qui concéptus est de Spíritu Sancto,
natus ex María Vírgine,
passus sub Póntio Piláto,
crucifíxus, mórtuus, et sepúltus;
descéndit ad inferos;
tértia die resurréxit a mórtuis;
ascéndit ad caelos;
sedet ad déxteram Dei Patris omnipoténtis;
inde ventúrus est iudicáre vivos et mórtuos.

Credo in Spíritum Sanctum,
sanctam Ecclésiam Cathólicam,
Sanctórum communiónem,
remissiónem peccatórum,
carnis resurrectiónem,
vitam aetérnam.
Amen.

The Prayer of the Faithful (Bidding Prayers)

Intentions will normally be for the Church; for the world; for those in particular need; and for the local community.

After each there is time for silent prayer, followed by the next intention, or concluded with a sung phrase such as

> **Christ, hear us,**
> *or* **Christ graciously hear us**,
>
> *or* *by a responsory such as:*
> Let us pray to the Lord.

R. **Grant this, almighty God.** *Or:*

R. **Lord, have mercy.** *Or:*

R. **Kyrie, eleison.**

The Priest concludes the Prayer with a collect.

The Liturgy of the Eucharist

For Catholics, the Eucharist is the source and summit of the whole Christian Life.

After the Liturgy of the Word, the people sit and the Offertory Chant begins. The faithful express their participation by making an offering, bringing forward bread and wine for the celebration of the Eucharist.

Preparatory Prayers

Standing at the altar, the Priest takes the paten with the bread and holds it slightly raised above the altar with both hands, saying:

Pr.   Blessed are you, Lord God of all creation,
for through your goodness we have received
the bread we offer you:
fruit of the earth and work of human hands,
it will become for us the bread of life.

R.   **Blessed be God for ever.**

The Priest then takes the chalice and holds it slightly raised above the altar with both hands, saying:

Pr.   Blessed are you, Lord God of all creation,
for through your goodness we have received
the wine we offer you:
fruit of the vine and work of human hands,
it will become our spiritual drink.

R.   **Blessed be God for ever.**

The Priest completes additional personal preparatory rites,
and the people rise as he says:

Pr. Pray, brethren (brothers and sisters),
that my sacrifice and yours
may be acceptable to God,
the almighty Father.

R. **May the Lord accept the sacrifice at your hands**
for the praise and glory of his name,
for our good
and the good of all his holy Church.

The Prayer over the Offerings

The Priest says the Prayer over the Offerings, at the end of
which the people acclaim:

R. **Amen.**

The Eucharistic Prayer

Extending his hands, the Priest says:

Pr. The Lord be with you.

R. **And with your spirit.**

Pr. Lift up your hearts.

R. **We lift them up to the Lord.**

Pr. Let us give thanks to the Lord our God.

R. **It is right and just.**

The Priest continues with the Preface appropriate to the season or feast at the end of which all sing or say:

Holy, Holy, Holy Lord God of hosts.
Heaven and earth are full of your glory.
Hosanna in the highest.
Blessed is he who comes in the name of the Lord.
Hosanna in the highest.

After the Sanctus the congregation kneels for the remainder of the Eucharistic Prayer.

Eucharistic Prayer I
(The Roman Canon)

Pr. To you, therefore, most merciful Father,
we make humble prayer and petition
through Jesus Christ, your Son, our Lord:
that you accept
and bless ✠ these gifts, these offerings,
these holy and unblemished sacrifices,
which we offer you firstly
for your holy catholic Church.
Be pleased to grant her peace,
to guard, unite and govern her
throughout the whole world,
together with your servant N. our Pope
and N. our Bishop,[1]
and all those who, holding to the truth,
hand on the catholic and apostolic faith.

Remember, Lord, your servants N. and N.
and all gathered here,
whose faith and devotion are known to you.
For them, we offer you this sacrifice of praise
or they offer it for themselves
and all who are dear to them:
for the redemption of their souls,
in hope of health and well-being,
and paying their homage to you,
the eternal God, living and true.

---

[1] Mention may be made here of the Coadjutor Bishop, or Auxiliary Bishops.

In communion with those whose memory we venerate,
especially the glorious ever-Virgin Mary,
Mother of our God and Lord, Jesus Christ,
† and blessed Joseph, her Spouse,
your blessed Apostles and Martyrs,
Peter and Paul, Andrew,
(James, John,
Thomas, James, Philip,
Bartholomew, Matthew,
Simon and Jude;
Linus, Cletus, Clement, Sixtus,
Cornelius, Cyprian,
Lawrence, Chrysogonus,
John and Paul,
Cosmas and Damian)
and all your Saints;
we ask that through their merits and prayers,
in all things we may be defended
by your protecting help.
(Through Christ our Lord. Amen.)

Therefore, Lord, we pray:
graciously accept this oblation of our service,
that of your whole family;
order our days in your peace,
and command that we be delivered
    from eternal damnation
and counted among the flock of those you have chosen.
(Through Christ our Lord. Amen.)

Be pleased, O God, we pray,
to bless, acknowledge,
and approve this offering in every respect;
make it spiritual and acceptable,
so that it may become for us
the Body and Blood of your most beloved Son,
our Lord Jesus Christ.

On the day before he was to suffer,
he took bread in his holy and venerable hands,
and with eyes raised to heaven
to you, O God, his almighty Father,
giving you thanks, he said the blessing,
broke the bread
and gave it to his disciples, saying:

TAKE THIS, ALL OF YOU, AND EAT OF IT,

 FOR THIS IS MY BODY,

WHICH WILL BE GIVEN UP FOR YOU.

In a similar way, when supper was ended,
he took this precious chalice
in his holy and venerable hands,
and once more giving you thanks, he said the blessing
and gave the chalice to his disciples, saying:

TAKE THIS, ALL OF YOU, AND DRINK FROM IT,

FOR THIS IS THE CHALICE OF MY BLOOD,

THE BLOOD OF THE NEW AND ETERNAL COVENANT,

WHICH WILL BE POURED OUT FOR YOU AND FOR MANY

FOR THE FORGIVENESS OF SINS.

 DO THIS IN MEMORY OF ME.

Pr.   The mystery of faith.

The people continue, acclaiming one of the following:

1. **We proclaim your Death, O Lord,**
   and profess your Resurrection
   until you come again.

2. **When we eat this Bread and drink this Cup,**
   we proclaim your Death, O Lord,
   until you come again.

3. **Save us, Saviour of the world,**
   for by your Cross and Resurrection
   you have set us free.

Pr. Therefore, O Lord,
as we celebrate the memorial of the blessed Passion,
the Resurrection from the dead,
and the glorious Ascension into heaven
of Christ, your Son, our Lord,
we, your servants and your holy people,
offer to your glorious majesty
from the gifts that you have given us,
this pure victim,
this holy victim,
this spotless victim,
the holy Bread of eternal life
and the Chalice of everlasting salvation.

Be pleased to look upon these offerings
with a serene and kindly countenance,
and to accept them,
as once you were pleased to accept
the gifts of your servant Abel the just,
the sacrifice of Abraham, our father in faith,
and the offering of your high priest Melchizedek,
a holy sacrifice, a spotless victim.

In humble prayer we ask you, almighty God:
command that these gifts be borne
by the hands of your holy Angel
to your altar on high
in the sight of your divine majesty,
so that all of us, who through this participation
    at the altar
receive the most holy Body and Blood of your Son,
may be filled with every grace and heavenly blessing.
(Through Christ our Lord. Amen.)

Remember also, Lord, your servants N. and N.,
who have gone before us with the sign of faith
and rest in the sleep of peace.
Grant them, O Lord, we pray,
and all who sleep in Christ,
a place of refreshment, light and peace.
(Through Christ our Lord. Amen.)

To us, also, your servants, who, though sinners,
hope in your abundant mercies,
graciously grant some share
and fellowship with your holy Apostles and Martyrs:
with John the Baptist, Stephen,
Matthias, Barnabas,
(Ignatius, Alexander,
Marcellinus, Peter,
Felicity, Perpetua,
Agatha, Lucy,
Agnes, Cecilia, Anastasia)
and all your Saints;
admit us, we beseech you,
into their company,
not weighing our merits,
but granting us your pardon,
through Christ our Lord.

Through whom
you continue to make all these good things, O Lord;
you sanctify them, fill them with life,
bless them, and bestow them upon us.

The Priest takes the chalice and the paten with the host:

Pr. Through him, and with him, and in him,
O God, almighty Father,
in the unity of the Holy Spirit,
all glory and honour is yours,
for ever and ever.
R. Amen.

Eucharistic Prayer II

Pr. The Lord be with you.

R. **And with your spirit.**

Pr. Lift up your hearts.

R. **We lift them up to the Lord.**

Pr. Let us give thanks to the Lord our God.

R. **It is right and just.**

Pr. It is truly right and just, our duty and our salvation,
always and everywhere to give you thanks,
   Father most holy,
through your beloved Son, Jesus Christ,
your Word through whom you made all things,
whom you sent as our Saviour and Redeemer,
incarnate by the Holy Spirit and born of the Virgin.

Fulfilling your will and gaining for you a holy people,
he stretched out his hands as he endured his Passion,
so as to break the bonds of death
   and manifest the resurrection.
And so, with the Angels and all the Saints
we declare your glory,
as with one voice we acclaim:

The people sing or say aloud the Sanctus as on page 125.

Pr. You are indeed Holy, O Lord,
the fount of all holiness.
Make holy, therefore, these gifts, we pray,
by sending down your Spirit upon them
like the dewfall,
so that they may become for us
the Body and ✠ Blood of our Lord Jesus Christ.

At the time he was betrayed
and entered willingly into his Passion,
he took bread and, giving thanks, broke it,
and gave it to his disciples, saying:

TAKE THIS, ALL OF YOU, AND EAT OF IT,

FOR THIS IS MY BODY,

WHICH WILL BE GIVEN UP FOR YOU.

In a similar way, when supper was ended,
he took the chalice
and, once more giving thanks,
he gave it to his disciples, saying:

TAKE THIS, ALL OF YOU, AND DRINK FROM IT,

FOR THIS IS THE CHALICE OF MY BLOOD,

THE BLOOD OF THE NEW AND ETERNAL COVENANT,

WHICH WILL BE POURED OUT FOR YOU AND FOR MANY

FOR THE FORGIVENESS OF SINS.

DO THIS IN MEMORY OF ME.

Pr. The mystery of faith.

The people continue with one of the acclamations on page 129.

Pr. Therefore, as we celebrate
the memorial of his Death and Resurrection,
we offer you, Lord,
the Bread of life and the Chalice of salvation,
giving thanks that you have held us worthy
to be in your presence and minister to you.

Humbly we pray
that, partaking of the Body and Blood of Christ,
we may be gathered into one by the Holy Spirit.

Remember, Lord, your Church,
spread throughout the world,
and bring her to the fullness of charity,
together with N. our Pope and N. our Bishop[2]
and all the clergy.

In Masses for the Dead, the following may be added:

Remember your servant N.,
whom you have called (today)
from this world to yourself.
Grant that he (she) who was united with your Son
    in a death like his,
may also be one with him in his Resurrection.

134

---

[2] Mention may be made here of the Coadjutor Bishop, or Auxiliary Bishops.

Remember also our brothers and sisters
who have fallen asleep in the hope of the resurrection,
and all who have died in your mercy:
welcome them into the light of your face.

Have mercy on us all,
we pray, that with the Blessed Virgin Mary,
    Mother of God,
with blessed Joseph, her Spouse,
with the blessed Apostles,
and all the Saints who have pleased you
    throughout the ages,
we may merit to be coheirs to eternal life,
and may praise and glorify you
through your Son, Jesus Christ.

The Priest takes the chalice and the paten with the host:

Through him, and with him, and in him,
O God, almighty Father,
in the unity of the Holy Spirit,
all glory and honour is yours,
for ever and ever.
R. Amen.

Eucharistic Prayer III

Pr. You are indeed Holy, O Lord,
and all you have created rightly gives you praise,
for through your Son our Lord Jesus Christ,
by the power and working of the Holy Spirit,
you give life to all things and make them holy,
and you never cease to gather a people to yourself, so
that from the rising of the sun to its setting
a pure sacrifice may be offered to your name.

Therefore, O Lord, we humbly implore you:
by the same Spirit graciously make holy
these gifts we have brought to you for consecration,
that they may become the Body and ✠ Blood
of your Son our Lord Jesus Christ,
at whose command we celebrate these mysteries.

For on the night he was betrayed
he himself took bread,
and, giving you thanks, he said the blessing,

broke the bread and gave it to his disciples, saying:

TAKE THIS, ALL OF YOU, AND EAT OF IT,

FOR THIS IS MY BODY,

WHICH WILL BE GIVEN UP FOR YOU.

In a similar way, when supper was ended,
he took the chalice,
and, giving you thanks, he said the blessing,
and gave the chalice to his disciples, saying:

TAKE THIS, ALL OF YOU, AND DRINK FROM IT,

FOR THIS IS THE CHALICE OF MY BLOOD

THE BLOOD OF THE NEW AND ETERNAL COVENANT,

WHICH WILL BE POURED OUT FOR YOU AND FOR MANY

FOR THE FORGIVENESS OF SINS.

DO THIS IN MEMORY OF ME.

Pr. The mystery of faith.

The people continue with one of the acclamations on page 129.

Pr. Therefore, O Lord, as we celebrate the memorial
of the saving Passion of your Son,
his wondrous Resurrection
and Ascension into heaven,
and as we look forward to his second coming,
we offer you in thanksgiving
this holy and living sacrifice.

137

Look, we pray, upon the oblation of your Church
and, recognising the sacrificial Victim by whose death
you willed to reconcile us to yourself,
grant that we, who are nourished
by the Body and Blood of your Son
and filled with his Holy Spirit,
may become one body, one spirit in Christ.

May he make of us
an eternal offering to you,
so that we may obtain an inheritance with your elect,
especially with the most Blessed Virgin Mary,
    Mother of God,
with blessed Joseph, her Spouse,
with your blessed Apostles and glorious Martyrs
(with Saint N.: *the Saint of the day or Patron Saint*)
and with all the Saints,
on whose constant intercession in your presence
we rely for unfailing help.

May this Sacrifice of our reconciliation,
we pray, O Lord,
advance the peace and salvation of all the world.
Be pleased to confirm in faith and charity
your pilgrim Church on earth,
with your servant N. our Pope and N. our Bishop,[3]
the Order of Bishops, all the clergy,
and the entire people you have gained for your own.

Listen graciously to the prayers of this family,
whom you have summoned before you:
in your compassion, O merciful Father,
gather to yourself all your children
scattered throughout the world.

† To our departed brothers and sisters
and to all who were pleasing to you
at their passing from this life,
give kind admittance to your kingdom.

There we hope to enjoy for ever the fullness
    of your glory
    through Christ our Lord,
through whom you bestow on the world all that is good.†

---

[3] Mention may be made here of the Coadjutor Bishop, or Auxiliary Bishops.

The Priest takes the chalice and the paten with the host:

Through him, and with him, and in him,
O God, almighty Father,
in the unity of the Holy Spirit,
all glory and honour is yours,
for ever and ever.
R. Amen.

Then follows the Communion Rite.

*When this Eucharistic Prayer is used in Masses for the Dead,
the following may be said:*

† Remember your servant N.
whom you have called (today)
from this world to yourself.
Grant that he (she) who was united with your Son
    in a death like his,
may also be one with him in his Resurrection,
when from the earth
he will raise up in the flesh those who have died,
and transform our lowly body
after the pattern of his own glorious body.
To our departed brothers and sisters, too,
and to all who were pleasing to you
at their passing from this life,
give kind admittance to your kingdom.
There we hope to enjoy for ever the fullness
    of your glory,
when you will wipe away every tear from our eyes.
For seeing you, our God, as you are,
we shall be like you for all the ages
and praise you without end,
(*He joins his hands*)
through Christ our Lord,
through whom you bestow on the world all that is good.†

Eucharistic Prayer IV

Pr. The Lord be with you.

R. And with your spirit.

Pr. Lift up your hearts.

R. We lift them up to the Lord.

Pr. Let us give thanks to the Lord our God.

R. It is right and just.

Pr. It is truly right to give you thanks,
truly just to give you glory, Father most holy,
for you are the one God living and true,
existing before all ages and abiding for all eternity,
dwelling in unapproachable light;
yet you, who alone are good, the source of life,
have made all that is,
so that you might fill your creatures with blessings
and bring joy to many of them by the glory of your light.

And so, in your presence are countless hosts of Angels,
who serve you day and night
and, gazing upon the glory of your face,
glorify you without ceasing.

With them we, too, confess your name in exultation,
giving voice to every creature under heaven,
as we acclaim:

The people sing or say aloud the Sanctus on page 125.

Pr. We give you praise, Father most holy,
for you are great
and you have fashioned all your works
in wisdom and in love.
You formed man in your own image
and entrusted the whole world to his care,
so that in serving you alone, the Creator,
he might have dominion over all creatures.
And when through disobedience
    he had lost your friendship,
you did not abandon him to the domain of death.
For you came in mercy to the aid of all,
so that those who seek might find you.
Time and again you offered them covenants
and through the prophets
taught them to look forward to salvation.

And you so loved the world, Father most holy,
that in the fullness of time
you sent your Only Begotten Son to be our Saviour.
Made incarnate by the Holy Spirit
and born of the Virgin Mary,
he shared our human nature in all things but sin.
To the poor he proclaimed the good news of salvation,
to prisoners, freedom,
and to the sorrowful of heart, joy.
To accomplish your plan,
he gave himself up to death,
and, rising from the dead,
he destroyed death and restored life.

And that we might live no longer for ourselves
but for him who died and rose again for us,
he sent the Holy Spirit from you, Father,
as the first fruits for those who believe,
so that, bringing to perfection his work in the world,
he might sanctify creation to the full.

Therefore, O Lord, we pray:
may this same Holy Spirit
graciously sanctify these offerings,
that they may become
the Body and ✠ Blood of our Lord Jesus Christ for the
celebration of this great mystery,
which he himself left us as an eternal covenant.

For when the hour had come
for him to be glorified by you, Father most holy,
having loved his own who were in the world,
he loved them to the end:
and while they were at supper, he took bread, blessed
and broke it, and gave it to his disciples, saying:

TAKE THIS, ALL OF YOU,

AND EAT OF IT,

FOR THIS IS MY BODY,

WHICH WILL BE GIVEN UP FOR YOU.

In a similar way, taking the chalice filled with the fruit
of the vine, he gave thanks, and gave the chalice to his
disciples, saying:

TAKE THIS, ALL OF YOU, AND DRINK FROM IT,

FOR THIS IS THE CHALICE OF MY BLOOD,

THE BLOOD OF THE NEW AND ETERNAL COVENANT,

WHICH WILL BE POURED OUT FOR YOU AND FOR MANY

FOR THE FORGIVENESS OF SINS.

DO THIS IN MEMORY OF ME.

Pr. The mystery of faith.

The people continue with one of the acclamations on page 129.

Pr. Therefore, O Lord,
as we now celebrate the memorial of our redemption,
we remember Christ's Death
and his descent to the realm of the dead,
we proclaim his Resurrection
and his Ascension to your right hand,
and, as we await his coming in glory,
we offer you his Body and Blood,
the sacrifice acceptable to you
which brings salvation to the whole world.

Look, O Lord, upon the Sacrifice
which you yourself have provided for your Church,
and grant in your loving kindness
to all who partake of this one Bread and one Chalice
that, gathered into one body by the Holy Spirit,
they may truly become a living sacrifice in Christ
to the praise of your glory.

Therefore, Lord, remember now
all for whom we offer this sacrifice:
especially your servant N. our Pope, N. our Bishop,[4]
and the whole Order of Bishops,
all the clergy,
those who take part in this offering,
those gathered here before you,
your entire people,
and all who seek you with a sincere heart.

Remember also
those who have died in the peace of your Christ
and all the dead,
whose faith you alone have known.

---

[4] Mention may be made here of the Coadjutor Bishop, or Auxiliary Bishops.

To all of us, your children,
grant, O merciful Father,
that we may enter into a heavenly inheritance
with the Blessed Virgin Mary, Mother of God,
with blessed Joseph, her Spouse,
and with your Apostles and Saints in your kingdom.
There, with the whole of creation,
freed from the corruption of sin and death,
may we glorify you through Christ our Lord,
through whom you bestow on the world all that is good.

The Priest takes the chalice and the paten with the host:

Through him, and with him, and in him,
O God, almighty Father,
in the unity of the Holy Spirit,
all glory and honour is yours,
for ever and ever.
R. Amen.

The Communion Rite

Eating and drinking together the Lord's Body and Blood in a paschal meal is the culmination of the Eucharist.

The Lord's Prayer

After the chalice and paten have been set down, the congregation stands and the Priest says:

Pr. At the Saviour's command
and formed by divine teaching,
we dare to say:

Pr. Præceptis salutáribus móniti,
et divína institutióne formati,
audémus dicere:

Together with the people, he continues:

**Our Father, who art in heaven,
hallowed be thy name;
thy kingdom come,
thy will be done on earth as it is in heaven.
Give us this day our daily bread,
and forgive us our trespasses,
as we forgive those who trespass against us;
and lead us not into temptation,
but deliver us from evil.**

**Pater noster, qui es in cælis;
sanctificétur nomen tuum;
advéniat regnum tuum;
fiat voluntas tua sicut in cælo, et in terra.
Panem nostrum cotidiánum da nobis hódie;
et dimítte nobis débita nostra,
sicut et nos dimíttimus debitóribus nostris;
et ne nos indúcas in tentatiónem;
sed líbera nos a malo.**

Pr. Deliver us, Lord, we pray, from every evil,
graciously grant peace in our days,
that, by the help of your mercy,
we may be always free from sin
and safe from all distress,
as we await the blessed hope
and the coming of our Saviour, Jesus Christ.

**R. For the kingdom,
the power and the glory are yours
now and for ever.**

The Peace

Pr. Lord Jesus Christ,
who said to your Apostles:
Peace I leave you, my peace I give you;
look not on our sins,
but on the faith of your Church,
and graciously grant her peace and unity
in accordance with your will.
Who live and reign for ever and ever.

R. Amen.

Pr. The peace of the Lord be with you always.

R. And with your spirit.

Then the Deacon, or the Priest, adds:

Pr. Let us offer each other the sign of peace.

And all offer one another the customary sign of peace.

Breaking of the Bread

Then the Priest takes the host, breaks it over the paten,
and places a small piece in the chalice, saying quietly:

Pr. May this mingling of the Body and Blood
of our Lord Jesus Christ bring eternal life
to us who receive it.

Meanwhile the following is sung or said:

> **Lamb of God, you take away the sins of the world,
> have mercy on us.**

> **Lamb of God, you take away the sins of the world,
> have mercy on us.**

> **Lamb of God, you take away the sins of the world,
> grant us peace.**

> **Agnus Dei, qui tollis peccáta mundi: miserére nobis.**

> **Agnus Dei, qui tollis peccáta mundi: miserére nobis.**

> **Agnus Dei, qui tollis peccáta mundi:
> dona nobis pacem.**

Invitation to Communion

All kneel. The Priest genuflects, takes the host and,
holding it slightly raised above the paten or above
the chalice says aloud:

Pr. Behold the Lamb of God,
behold him who takes away the sins of the world.
Blessed are those called to the supper
of the Lamb.

R. **Lord, I am not worthy
that you should enter under my roof,
but only say the word
and my soul shall be healed.**

While the Priest is receiving the Body of Christ,
the Communion Chant begins.

Communion Procession

After the Priest has reverently consumed the Body and Blood of Christ he takes the paten or ciborium and approaches the communicants.

The Priest raises a host slightly and shows it to each of the communicants, saying:

Pr. The Body of Christ.

R. Amen.

When Communion is ministered from the chalice:

Pr. The Blood of Christ.

R. Amen.

After the distribution of Communion, if appropriate, a sacred silence may be observed for a while, or a psalm or other canticle of praise or a hymn may be sung. Then, the Priest says:

Pr. Let us pray.

Prayer after Communion

All stand and pray in silence for a while, unless silence has just been observed. Then the Priest says the Prayer after Communion, at the end of which the people acclaim:

R. Amen.

The Concluding Rites

The Mass closes, sending the faithful forth to put what they have celebrated into effect in their daily lives.

Any brief announcements follow here. Then the Dismissal takes place.

Pr. The Lord be with you.

R. And with your spirit.

The Priest blesses the people, saying:

Pr. May almighty God bless you,
the Father, and the Son, ✠ and the Holy Spirit.

R. Amen.

Then the Deacon, or the Priest himself says the Dismissal:

Pr. Go forth, the Mass is ended.

R. Thanks be to God. *Or:*

Pr. Go and announce the Gospel of the Lord.

R. Thanks be to God. *Or:*

Pr. Go in peace, glorifying the Lord by your life.

R. Thanks be to God. *Or:*

Pr. Go in peace.

R. Thanks be to God.

Then the Priest venerates the altar as at the beginning.

After making a profound bow with the ministers, he withdraws.

IF YOU CAN'T
GET TO MASS

Spiritual Communion

Spiritual Communion is the heartfelt desire to receive Our Lord, even when we are unable because of the distance or for some other reason. This desire to receive him through spiritual Communion is an act of love which prolongs our thanksgiving even when we are not in the Eucharistic presence of Our Lord. The wish to live constantly in his presence can be fuelled by acts of love and desire to be united with him and is a means of drawing more deeply from the life of the Holy Spirit dwelling within our souls in the state of grace. "The effects of a sacrament can be received by desire. Although in such a case the sacrament is not received physically ... nevertheless the actual reception of the sacrament itself brings with it fuller effect than receiving it through desire alone" (*St Thomas Aquinas*). The writings of the saints reveal many formulae for making a spiritual Communion:

Acts of Spiritual Communion

My Jesus, I believe that you are truly present
in the Most Holy Sacrament.
I love you above all things,
and I desire to receive you into my soul.
Since I cannot at this moment
    receive you sacramentally,
come at least spiritually into my heart.
I embrace you as being already there
    and unite myself wholly to you.
Never permit me to be separated from you.
Amen.

(St Alphonsus Liguori)

I wish, my Lord, to receive you with the purity,
humility and devotion with which your
Most Holy Mother received you,
with the spirit and fervour of the saints.

Give me, good Lord,
a longing to be with you…
give me warmth, delight and quickness
    in thinking upon you.
And give me your grace to long
    for your holy sacraments,
and specially to rejoice in the presence
    of your very blessed Body,
sweet Saviour Christ,
in the Holy Sacrament of the altar.

(St Thomas More)

PRAYERS FOR HOLY COMMUNION

Say these prayers slowly, a few words at a time. It is well to stop after every few words, that they may sink into the heart. Each prayer may be said several times.

Prayer before Mass

O God, to whom every heart is open,
every desire known and from whom
no secrets are hidden;
purify the thoughts of our hearts
by the inspiration of your Holy Spirit,
that we may perfectly love you,
and worthily praise your holy name.
Amen.

Before Holy Communion

Prayer for Help

O God, help me to make a good Communion.
Mary, my dearest mother,
pray to Jesus for me.
My dear Angel Guardian,
lead me to the Altar of God.

Act of Faith

O God, because you have said it,
I believe that I shall receive
the Sacred Body of Jesus Christ to eat,
and his Precious Blood to drink.
My God, I believe this with all my heart.

Act of Humility

My God, I confess that I am a poor sinner;
I am not worthy to receive
the Body and Blood of Jesus,
   on account of my sins.
Lord, I am not worthy to receive you under my roof;
but only say the word, and my soul will be healed.

Act of Sorrow

My God, I detest all the sins of my life.
I am sorry for them,
because they have offended you, my God,
you who are so good.
I resolve never to commit sin any more.
My good God, pity me, have mercy on me, forgive me.

Act of Adoration

O Jesus, great God, present on the Altar,
I bow down before you.
I adore you.

Act of Love and Desire

Jesus, I love you.
I desire with all my heart to receive you.
Jesus, come into my poor soul,
and give me your Flesh to eat and your Blood to drink.
Give me your whole Self, Body, Blood, Soul and Divinity,
that I may live for ever with you.

Prayer of St Thomas Aquinas

Almighty and ever-living God,
I approach the sacrament
of your only-begotten Son,
our Lord Jesus Christ.
I come sick to the doctor of life,
unclean to the fountain of mercy,
blind to the radiance of eternal light,
poor and needy to the Lord of heaven and earth.
Lord in your great generosity, heal my sickness,
wash away my defilement, enlighten my blindness,
enrich my poverty, and clothe my nakedness.

May I receive the bread of angels,
the King of kings and Lord of lords,
with humble reverence, with purity and faith,
with repentance and love and the determined purpose
that will help to bring me to salvation.
May I receive the sacrament of the Lord's body
and blood and its reality and power.
Kind God, may I receive the body
of your only begotten Son, our Lord Jesus Christ, born
from the womb of the Virgin Mary,
and so be received into his mystical body
and numbered among his members.
Loving Father, as on my earthly pilgrimage
I now receive your beloved Son under the veil
of a sacrament,
may I one day see him face to face in glory,
who lives and reigns with you for ever.
Amen.

Receiving Holy Communion

When the priest or minister says "The Body of Christ", answer "Amen" and receive the sacred host with reverence. If you receive Holy Communion in the hand, place the host reverently into your mouth before returning to your place. If Holy Communion is given from the chalice, answer "Amen" when the priest or minister says "The Blood of Christ"; take the chalice and drink a little of the Precious Blood, taking care not to spill any. Say in your heart, with all the faith of St Thomas "My Lord and my God". Jesus is now really present in you. Keep away all earthly thoughts and enjoy his presence.

After Holy Communion

I give you thanks

I give you thanks, Lord, Holy Father, everlasting God.
In your great mercy,
and not because of my own merits,
you have fed me a sinner and your unworthy servant,
with the precious body and blood of your Son,
our Lord Jesus Christ.
I pray that this Holy Communion may not serve
as my judgement and condemnation,
but as my forgiveness and salvation.
May it be my armour of faith and shield of good purpose,
root out in me all that is evil and increase every virtue.
I beseech you to bring me a sinner,
to that great feast where,
with your Son and the Holy Spirit you are the true light
of your holy ones,
their flawless blessedness,
everlasting joy and perfect happiness.
Through Christ our Lord.
Amen.

(St Thomas Aquinas)

Act of Faith

O Jesus, I believe that I have received your Flesh
to eat and your Blood to drink,
because you have said it,
and your word is true.
All that I have and all that I am are your gift
and now you have given me yourself.

Act of Adoration

O Jesus, my God, my Creator, I adore you,
because from your hands I came and with you
I am to be happy for ever.

Act of Humility

O Jesus, I am not worthy to receive you,
and yet you have come to me that my poor heart
may learn of you to be meek and humble.

Act of Love

J esus, I love you;
I love you with all my heart.
You know that I love you,
and wish to love you daily more and more.

Act of Thanksgiving

M y good Jesus, I thank you with all my heart.
How good, how kind you are to me.
Blessed be Jesus
in the most holy Sacrament of the Altar.

Act of Offering

O Jesus, receive my poor offering. Jesus, you have given yourself to me, and now let me give myself to you: I give you my body, that I may be chaste and pure. I give you my soul, that I may be free from sin. I give you my heart, that I may always love you. I give you my every breath that I shall breathe, and especially my last. I give you myself in life and in death, that I may be yours for ever and ever.

For Yourself

O Jesus, wash away my sins
with your Precious Blood.
O Jesus, the struggle against temptation
   is not yet finished.
My Jesus, when temptation comes near me,
make me strong against it.
In the moment of temptation may I always say:
"My Jesus, mercy! Mary, help!"
O Jesus, may I lead a good life;
may I die a happy death.
May I receive you before I die.
May I say when I am dying:
"Jesus, Mary and Joseph, I give you my heart and my soul".

Listen now for a moment to Jesus Christ; perhaps he has
something to say to you. Answer Jesus in your heart,
and tell him all your troubles. Then say:

For Perseverance

Jesus, I am going away for a time,
but I trust not without you.
You are with me by your grace.
I resolve never to leave you by mortal sin.
Although I am so weak I have such hope in you.
Give me grace to persevere. Amen.

A VISIT TO
THE BLESSED
SACRAMENT

Sitting or kneeling before Jesus truly present in the Blessed Sacrament, it may be helpful to reflect on the love and tenderness of our Lord, by meditating upon this (or another) passage of Scripture:

"No one can come to me unless he is drawn by the Father who sent me, and I will raise him up at the last day. It is written in the prophets: They will all be taught by God, and to hear the teaching of the Father, and learn from it, is to come to me. Not that anybody has seen the Father, except the one who comes from God: he has seen the Father. I tell you most solemnly, everybody who believes has eternal life. I am the bread of life. Your fathers ate the manna in the desert and they are dead; but this is the bread that comes down from heaven, so that a man may eat it and not die. I am the living bread which has come down from heaven.

"Anyone who eats this bread will live for ever; and the bread that I shall give is my flesh, for the life of the world." Then the Jews started arguing with one another: "How can this man give us his flesh to eat?" they said. Jesus replied: "I tell you most solemnly, if you do not eat the flesh of the Son of Man and drink his blood, you will not have life in you. Anyone who does eat my flesh and drink my blood has eternal life, and I shall raise him up on the last day.

"For my flesh is real food and my blood is real drink. He who eats my flesh and drinks my blood lives in me and I live in him. As I, who am sent by the living Father, myself draw life from the Father, so whoever eats me will draw life from me.

"This is the bread come down from heaven; not like the bread our ancestors ate: they are dead, but anyone who eats this bread will live for ever."

(John 6:44-58)

THE MASS
SIMPLY EXPLAINED

"At the Last Supper, on the night he was betrayed, our Saviour instituted the Eucharistic sacrifice of his Body and Blood. This he did in order to perpetuate the sacrifice of the Cross throughout the ages until he should come again, and so to entrust to his beloved Spouse, the Church, a memorial of his death and Resurrection: a sacrament of love, a sign of unity, a bond of charity, a Paschal banquet 'in which Christ is consumed, the mind is filled with grace, and a pledge of future glory is given to us'" (*Catechism* 1323).

First we come together in one place to celebrate the Eucharist in communion with the whole Church. At our head is Christ, the High Priest. The bishop or priest acts in the person of Christ.

The word of God in the inspired Scriptures is proclaimed. The homily encourages us to accept this word and to put it into practice. In the intercessions, we pray for the Church, for the world, for those in need and for local needs.

The offerings of bread and wine are placed upon the altar and offered by the priest in the name of Christ. The Creator's gifts are placed into the hands of Christ who, in his sacrifice perfects all human attempts to offer sacrifice.

The Eucharistic Prayer is the heart and summit of the whole celebration. The priest gives thanks to God in the preface and we praise him in union with the angels and saints. The priest asks the Father to send the Holy Spirit upon the gifts of bread and wine so that they truly become the Body and Blood of Jesus Christ. His one, eternal sacrifice offered for us upon the Cross is made present. The Church calls to mind the Passion, death and Resurrection of Christ, which are made present in the Eucharist. The prayer reminds us that we offer the

Eucharist in communion with the Bishop of Rome, the local bishop and the whole Church throughout the world.

In Holy Communion, we share in the sacred and heavenly banquet and receive the body and blood of Christ as the "bread of heaven" and the "chalice of salvation", the food and life of our souls (*Catechism* 1346).

Who may receive Holy Communion?

To receive Holy Communion, we must be "in communion" with the Church: we should be in a state of grace, keep the fast of one hour (not required for the elderly or sick), and we should prepare devoutly to receive the sacrament.

The Church encourages those who are properly disposed to receive Holy Communion whenever they participate in the Mass.

Those who are living together as husband and wife but who are not married, or who are married outside the Church without permission may not receive Holy Communion.

If we are conscious of having committed a mortal sin, we should make a sacramental confession before receiving Holy Communion.

The Sunday Obligation

The first commandment of the Church binds all Catholics to attend Mass on all Sundays and Holy Days of Obligation.

This is a grave obligation on our conscience, unless some really serious cause prevents us. To come in late, wilfully or through carelessness, when Mass has begun, is at least a venial sin. To miss Mass when you cannot help it, or when it would be very difficult for you to attend Mass, is not a sin. So, if you were to miss Mass because you were ill, or because you had to stay at home to mind a sick person or children, or because you were a very long way from church, or if for some other reason you could not go, it would not be a sin. When you cannot go to Mass, say the Mass prayers yourself at home, if possible.

Fasting and Abstinence

The age at which abstinence becomes binding is fourteen. The obligation of fasting is restricted to those who have completed their eighteenth year and it continues until they have begun their sixtieth.

Fasting and abstinence are binding throughout the Church on Ash Wednesday and Good Friday.

The law of the Church requires Catholics on Fridays to abstain from meat, or some other form of food, or to observe some form of penance laid down by the local Bishops' Conference. (*Code of Canon Law* 1251)

The Bishops of England and Wales have decided that in England and Wales this penance should be fulfilled simply by abstaining from meat and by uniting this to prayer. Those who cannot or choose not to eat meat as part of their normal diet should abstain from some other food of which they regularly partake.

The Eucharistic Fast

1. Water (and medicine) may be taken at any time.
2. Solid food and drinks may be taken up to one hour before Holy Communion.
3. Those who are advanced in age or who suffer from any infirmity, as well as those who take care of them, can receive Holy Communion even if they have taken something during the previous hour.

Note on Indulgences

An indulgence is a remission before God of the temporal punishment due to sins whose guilt has already been forgiven, which the faithful Christian who is duly disposed gains under certain prescribed conditions through the action of the Church which, as the minister of redemption, dispenses and applies with authority the treasury of the satisfactions of Christ and the saints. An indulgence is partial or plenary according as it removes either part or all of the temporal punishment due to sin. The faithful can gain indulgences for themselves or apply them to the dead.

To understand this doctrine and practice of the Church, it is necessary to understand that sin has a double consequence. Grave sin deprives us of communion with God and therefore makes us incapable of eternal life, the privation of which is called the "eternal punishment" of sin. On the other hand every sin, even venial, entails an unhealthy attachment to creatures, which must be purified either here on earth, or after death in the state called purgatory. This purification frees one from what is called the "temporal punishment" of sin. These two punishments must not be conceived of as a kind of vengeance inflicted by God from without, but as following from the very nature of sin (*Catechism* 1471-2).

To gain a plenary indulgence it is necessary to perform the work to which the indulgence is attached and to fulfil the following three conditions:

Sacramental Confession,

Holy Communion,

Prayer for the intention of the Holy Father.

It is further required that all attachment to sin, even venial sin, be absent. If this disposition is in any way less than perfect or if the prescribed three conditions are not fulfilled, the indulgence will be partial only.

The condition of praying for the intention of the Sovereign Pontiff is fully satisfied by reciting one Our Father and one Hail Mary; nevertheless, each one is free to recite any other prayer according to his piety and devotion.

A partial indulgence is granted to the faithful who:

1. In the performance of their duties and in bearing the trials of life, raise their mind with humble confidence to God, adding - even if only mentally - some pious invocation.

2. In a spirit of faith and mercy give of themselves or of their goods to serve their brothers in need.

3. In a spirit of penance voluntarily deprive themselves of what is licit and pleasing to them.

For specific prayers and devotions

The Holy Rosary: A plenary indulgence, for the recitation of the Rosary (five decades), in a church or public oratory or in the family. If said privately, a partial indulgence.

The Way of the Cross: A plenary indulgence.

Prayer before a Crucifix: A plenary indulgence, on the Fridays in Lent and Passiontide. At other times a partial indulgence.

Act of Resignation: A partial indulgence. A plenary indulgence at the hour of death, if properly disposed and in the habit of reciting some prayers.

PREPARING TO PARTICIPATE IN THE MASS

Preparing to celebrate

"To prepare ourselves to celebrate the sacred mysteries."

We must prepare our minds and hearts for the celebration of Mass. "We live today in a society in which every space, every moment must be 'filled' with initiatives, activities and sound, so that there is no time for listening and dialogue. Dear brothers and sisters, don't be afraid of silence outside and inside ourselves, if we want to hear not only the voice of God but also of those who are close to us, the voices of others." (Pope Benedict XVI)

Unnecessary conversation both before and after the celebration of the sacred liturgy disturbs an atmosphere which is conducive to prayer and worship. Let us take to heart the poetical words of St John Chrysostom (347-407): "the church is the dwelling of angels; it is the kingdom of God; it is heaven itself so in the church let only spiritual things be spoken."

As we enter the church and pass through the door let us recall the words of the Lord: "I am the door" (*John* 10:9). We bless ourselves with Holy Water as a reminder "of the Sacrament of Baptism, through which we become sharers in the death and Resurrection of Jesus Christ." (Pope Benedict XVI)

Through our genuflection to the Blessed Sacrament we acknowledge that have come into the presence of the Lord and proclaim our faith in the real presence. We then take our place as members of "a chosen race, a royal priesthood, a holy nation" and prepare ourselves to celebrate the sacred mysteries.

Behaviour

*"Let us consider how we ought to behave
in the presence of God."*

(St Benedict)

"A liturgical celebration is always a very serious action. It must be prepared and carried out with great care in its every detail." (Pope Paul VI) Care for external details must be accompanied by attention to internal dispositions. To be attentive to gestures and postures makes an important contribution towards creating that atmosphere of recollection which is felt by many to be lacking in our liturgy.

Standing is a mark of respect. We stand to sing God's praises and to pray for our needs and those of all peoples on the earth. Standing is also a sign of waiting in readiness for the Lord. To stand up is to give witness and make an affirmation; that is why we stand to profess our faith.

Kneeling is a sign of penitence and a gesture of supplication. It is a powerful symbol of adoration and of acknowledgement of our dependence upon the Lord our God, Creator of heaven and earth. It is a gesture which we find frequently in Scripture and it has an important place in the liturgy.

The profound bow is a deep sign of reverence. A profound bow is made when passing in front of the altar and during the Creed. The bowing of the head is a sign of reverence.

Sitting is a position for listening and learning, just as Mary of Bethany sat at the Lord's feet and listened to his teaching. We sit to listen to the word of God and to ponder it in our hearts in prayer.

When we walk in procession we are reminded that we are the pilgrim people of God.

The House of the Lord

Where Christians gather to celebrate the sacred mysteries are found the altar, ambo and the chair of the one who presides at the assembly.

The Altar

The altar is the place on which the sacrifice of the Cross is made present and it is the holy table of the Lord to which we have been invited.

Enough emphasis has not been laid upon the holiness and sacred character of the altar. To the altar we bring ourselves, our offerings and prayers of petition, praise and thanksgiving. Devotion to the altar is founded upon the mystery which is celebrated there: "May this altar be the place where the great mysteries of redemption are accomplished: a place where your people offer their gifts, unfold their good intentions, pour out their prayers, and echo every meaning of their faith and devotion." (Prayer from Rite of the Dedication of an Altar)

The Ambo

The place from which the Word of God is proclaimed is called by the Fathers of the Church "a throne for the word of God and the seat of wisdom". It is by hearing the word and sharing in the bread of life that we grow into the full stature of Christ.

The Chair

The Eucharist is the action of Christ and the people of God hierarchically assembled. The president's chair is a sign of his ministry of service in imitation of the Lord who came not to be served but to serve and give himself for us.

The Structure of the Mass

"We must learn to understand the structure of the liturgy and why it is laid out as it is."

(Pope Benedict XVI)

The essential elements in the structure of the Mass have remained unchanged from the time of the Apostles.

There have been developments and enrichments in the form of the Mass but as Pope Benedict remarked: "The liturgy which developed in the course of two millenniums has always remained a continuation of ongoing growth of worship and proclamation."

There are two parts in the Mass that make up one single act of worship: the Liturgy of the Word and the Liturgy of the Eucharist.

The Liturgy of the Word is made up of the proclamation of readings from Holy Scripture, the homily, the Creed, (on Sundays and Solemnities) and ends with the Bidding Prayers.

The Liturgy of the Eucharist begins with the procession and presentation of the bread and wine for the holy sacrifice. When the prayer over the Gifts has been said the celebrant begins the Eucharistic Prayer. After the Great Amen at the end of the Eucharistic Prayer the preparation for Holy Communion begins with the Our Father and the prayer for the peace and unity of the Church. While the hymn Lamb of God is sung, there takes place the ancient and sacred gesture of the "breaking of the bread". After Communion and thanksgiving the Liturgy of the Eucharist is brought to a close with the prayer after Communion.

As is fitting, these two parts of the Mass, Word and Sacrament, are preceded by an introduction and followed by a conclusion.

The introductory rites are: the entrance chant and the veneration of the altar, followed by the greeting, the Act of Penance, the Lord have mercy, the Glory to God (when prescribed), and the Collect Prayer which concludes the introductory rites.

The Mass ends with the concluding rites which consist of the final greeting and blessing, followed by the dismissal, the veneration of the altar and the out-going procession.

Once we have grasped the structure of the liturgy and its various parts we must make it our own. "We must interiorise the structure, the words of the liturgy, the Word of God. By doing this, our celebration truly becomes a celebration 'with' the Church. Our hearts are enlarged and we are not doing just anything but are 'with' the Church, in conversation with God." (Pope Benedict XVI)

The Introductory Rites

"Where two or three are gathered in my name, there am I in the midst of them."

(Matthew 18:20)

The Introductory Rites help the congregation to become "one mind and heart", ready to listen attentively to the proclamation of the word of God and to participate in celebration of the holy Eucharist.

Entrance Chant

The entrance chant accompanies the procession of the Celebrant and ministers to the altar and helps to introduce the assembly to the season, feast or mystery that is being celebrated.

Veneration of the Altar and Greeting of the People

As the Celebrant and the ministers reach the place of celebration, they make a sign of honour and reverence to Blessed Sacrament and to the altar. The Celebrant and the ordained ministers venerate the altar with a kiss. On Sundays and Feast Days incense may be used. The Celebrant takes the censer from the Deacon or server and walks around the altar incensing it. If the Celebrant passes in front of the Cross he reverences it with incense.

The smoke rising from the censer is a symbol of the prayers of the people of God that ascend to heaven.

Sign of the Cross

"We should glory in the Cross of our Lord Jesus Christ, for He is our salvation, our life and our resurrection."

Opening Chant for the Feast of the Exaltation of the Holy Cross

Our opening words and gesture are an affirmation of our baptismal profession of faith in God: Father, Son and Holy Spirit. They also remind us that we have been called to bear witness by our lives to the Gospel: "Go, therefore, and make disciples of all nations, baptising them in the name of the Father and of the Son and of the Holy Spirit" (*Matthew* 28:19).

Amen is an ancient Hebrew word which means giving approval for what has been said or done. Amen is always a decisive and definitive affirmation: "so be it for it cannot be otherwise". Whenever Amen occurs in the liturgy it always has this meaning of giving assent to what has been said and accomplished.

Greeting

When the Risen Lord appeared to the disciples in the upper room he immediately greeted them: "Peace be with you". Following his example the Celebrant greets those who are assembled in the name of Christ Jesus. It is not only inappropriate to use a form of secular greeting, such as "good morning", but shows a misunderstanding of what it means to be gathered in the name of the Lord.

If there is a need for a special word of welcome this must come after the greeting.

We have several forms of greeting but all are taken from Holy Scripture and are among our oldest liturgical texts.

The greetings express what St Paul wrote to the Philippians and form a fitting preparation to our celebration. "Do not be anxious about anything, but in everything, by prayer and petition, with thanksgiving, present your requests to God. And the peace of God, which transcends all understanding, will guard your hearts and your minds in Christ Jesus."

In his greeting the Celebrant also prays that "communion of the Holy Spirit" be with us. The word communion expresses the nature of the Church. The most fundamental fellowship is not with one another, but is our communion in the life of Christ. Through the communion of the Holy Spirit we become one body, one spirit in Christ. Our fellowship in the bond of charity is the fruit of communion.

"The Church is called during her earthly pilgrimage to maintain and promote communion with the Triune God and communion among the faithful. For this purpose she possesses the word and the sacraments, particularly the Eucharist, by which she 'constantly lives and grows' and in which she expresses her very nature." (Pope St John Paul II).

The greeting "Grace to you and peace" is found in the oldest of the New Testament writings, the first Letter of St Paul to the Thessalonians, written about the year 55. It is wonderful that these words still find a place in our celebration of the liturgy. The greeting "The Lord be with you" is the simplest and the most ancient of greetings. It expresses the wish that the faithful should be with the Lord and under Divine protection in order to grow into the fulness of the stature of Christ.

When the bishop celebrates he says: "Peace be with you". This is the greeting used by the risen Lord to his disciples gathered in the upper room. These words are also a proclamation and affirmation that here in this place the mystery of the Church is made manifest.

And with your spirit

The reply of the people to all the greetings is: And with your spirit. There are several expressions in the New Testament that are of Hebrew or Aramaic origin and which have remained in their original language. By continuing to use these words we retain a direct link with the beginnings of Christianity. "And with your spirit" was frequently used by St Paul. To the Galatians he wrote "May the grace of our Lord Jesus Christ be with your spirit" (*Galatians* 6:18). With greater simplicity he greeted Timothy with the words, "the Lord be with your spirit" (2 *Timothy* 4:22). The response "And with your spirit", shows that the priest is not acting in his own name but that his ministry is from God and does not depend upon his human qualities and gifts. It reminds the priest of the great responsibility he has undertaken through ordination. The great Doctor of the Church, St John Chrysostom, told his congregation that by saying "and with your spirit" they were showing that they understood that the bishop celebrates the holy sacrifice, not in his own name, but in the power of the Holy Spirit.

The Act of Penitence

After the greeting the Priest invites all present to participate in a Penitential Act so that our hearts and minds may be made ready to celebrate the sacred mysteries.

To acknowledge our sin is a sign of trust in the mercy of God. St Cyprian in his commentary on the Lord's Prayer wrote: "When the publican prayed with the Pharisee in the Temple he did not lift up his eyes boldly to heaven, nor proudly raise his hands; but beating his breast, and testifying to the sins shut up within, he implored the help of the divine mercy".

An ancient document called "The Teaching of the Apostles" written about the year 95 tells Christians: "On the Lord's day gather together, break bread and give thanks after confessing your transgressions so that your sacrifice may be pure".

We have come into the presence of the Lord giving thanks and, by acknowledging our sin, we also give thanks for his gracious love and mercy because we know that the Lord is good and forgiving and that he will grant us his gift of pardon and peace.

Through my most grievous fault

In Holy Scripture striking one's breast is a way of showing profound sorrow for having offended God. The repetition of "through my fault" is meant to convey the sincerity of the words expressing repentance.

Signs and symbols are an integral part of the liturgy and therefore body language, such as striking the breast, standing, kneeling and bowing have a significant place in our celebrations.

After each of the various forms of the Penitential Act the celebrant invokes the mercy of God so that with our sins forgiven we may be admitted to the heavenly kingdom.

Lord, have mercy

With these words the faithful acclaim the Lord is God and implore his mercy. This ancient prayer was introduced into the Roman rite at the end of the fifth century by Pope Gelasius I who died in 496.

Glory to God in the highest

This is an ancient Greek hymn with which the Church, gathered in the Holy Spirit, glorifies and praises God. The opening words are from the Gospel of St Luke (2:13-14) "There was with the angel a multitude of the heavenly host praising God and saying, 'Glory to God in the highest, and on earth peace to people of good will'". "This joyful hymn calls upon the faithful to celebrate the glory of God, Father, Son, and Holy Spirit: 'You alone are the Most High, Jesus Christ, with the Holy Spirit, in the glory of God the Father'.

"This angelic song has been recognised from the earliest days as music proceeding from God, indeed, as an invitation to join in the singing with hearts filled with joy at the fact that we are loved by God. St Augustine says that singing is a mark of one who loves. Thus, down the centuries, the angels' song has again and again become a song of love and joy, a song of those who love." (Pope Benedict XVI)

The Collect

These words, Let us pray, remind us that "Our prayer is public and common; and when we pray, we pray not for one, but for the whole people, because we the whole people are one." (St Cyprian)

The Liturgy of the Word

When the Sacred Scriptures are read to us it is God who speaks to us and through these sacred readings we are nourished at the table of God's word. The image of the two tables, the Word of God and the Eucharist, is found in the teaching of the great Fathers of the Church. "From the table of the Lord we receive the bread of life… And from the table of Sunday readings we are nourished with the doctrine of the Lord." (St Augustine)

"There are two tables in the treasures of the Church. One is the table of the holy altar on which rests a consecrated bread, the precious body of Jesus Christ. The other is the table of the divine Law." (*The Imitation of Christ*).

The Word of the Lord

After each reading the assembled people by their acclamation "Thanks be to God" show that they have heard and welcomed the Word of God in faith and with gratitude.

The Responsorial psalm which follows the reading is a prayerful meditation on the word of God.

The Gospel

"We have a custom of singing Alleluia which is an old tradition of the Church: in this word is signified the praise of God" (St Augustine). Through this acclamation the faithful welcome and greet the Lord who is about to speak to them in the Gospel.

The Gospel book is carried in procession to the place of its proclamation, accompanied by candles and incense. Such marks of reverence help to prepare the minds and hearts of all present as they stand to listen to the holy reading.

"When the Gospel is to be read at Mass, stand up to show that you are ready and equipped to walk on the way that the Gospel commands." (St Francis de Sales)

Glory to you, O Lord

"Let us therefore hear the Gospel just as if we were listening to the Lord himself present" (St Augustine). We make the Sign of the Cross on our forehead, lips, and breast to expresses the desire that the words of the Holy Gospel should be in our mind, in our mouth, and in our heart.

Praise to you, Lord Jesus Christ

These words affirm our faith that through the power of the Holy Spirit, the Lord is present to us in the proclamation of the Gospel.

The Gospel is always a call to conversion, "repent and believe in the Gospel", so it is fitting that the kissing of the book be accompanied by the prayer: "Through the words of the Gospel may our sins be wiped away".

The Homily

"The homily is a means of bringing the scriptural message to life in a way that helps the faithful to realise that God's word is present and at work in their everyday lives. It should lead to an understanding of the mystery being celebrated, serve as a summons to mission, and prepare the assembly for the profession of faith, the universal prayer and the Eucharistic liturgy." (Pope Benedict XVI)

The Creed: Profession of Faith

The profession of faith prepares us for the celebration of the sacred mysteries. "The Creed is not a collection of propositions; it is not a theory. In the mystery of baptism, God comes close to us and brings us closer to one another…we say: 'I believe in God the Father, the Creator of heaven and earth'. We believe that at the beginning of everything is the eternal Word. With this faith we have no reason to fear. We rejoice that we can know God!" (Pope Benedict XVI)

The Apostles' Creed

The Apostles' Creed may be used during Lent and Easter Time. "The Church, for her part, has given us a summary of faith in which everything essential is expressed. It is the 'Apostles' Creed', which is divided into twelve articles, corresponding to the number of the twelve Apostles. It speaks of God, the creator and source of all that is, of Christ and his work of salvation, and it culminates in the resurrection of the dead and life everlasting." (Pope Benedict XVI)

The Prayer of the Faithful or Bidding Prayers

St Paul wrote to his disciple Timothy that there should be "prayers, petitions, intercessions and thanksgiving for all: for rulers and all in authority, so that we may be able to live quiet and peaceful lives in the full practice of religion and of morality" (*1 Timothy* 2:1-4). With these prayers the faithful exercise their baptismal priestly function, by interceding for the needs of all peoples on the earth.

The Liturgy of the Eucharist

The presentation of the gifts

"In the bread and wine that we bring to the altar, all creation is taken up by Christ the Redeemer to be transformed and presented to the Father. In this way we also bring to the altar all the pain and suffering of the world, in the certainty that everything has value in God's eyes. God invites us to participate in bringing to fulfilment his handiwork, and in so doing, gives human labour its authentic meaning, since, through the celebration of the Eucharist, it is united to the redemptive sacrifice of Christ." (Pope Benedict XVI)

The corporal, purificator, chalice, pall, and the Missal are placed on the altar. The faithful express their participation by making an offering and bringing forward bread and wine for the celebration of the Eucharist.

Blessed are you, Lord, God of all creation

The bread and wine are a symbol of the earth's produce and our life and work. They come to us through the goodness of God our Father from whom every good gift comes. These humble gifts, the fruit of the earth and work of human hands, will become for us the bread of life and our spiritual drink.

Wine and a little water are poured into the chalice with the words: By the mystery of this water and wine may we come to share in the divinity of Christ who humbled himself to share in our humanity.

The mingling of a little water with wine was the normal practice at the time of our Lord. This prayer praises God for the great mystery of the Incarnation whereby through his sharing in our human nature, Christ Jesus gave us a share in his divine nature. According to St Cyprian the practice of mingling water with wine was "according to the tradition of the Lord". For the holy bishop the drop of water was a sign that the Church was participating in the sacrifice of Christ. The wine represents Christ our Lord and the water the people whom he redeemed through his precious blood and washed clean in the waters of baptism.

The prayer of a "humble spirit and contrite heart" is acceptable to God (Psalm 51: 19) and so the priest prays that through our humble prayer, our sacrifice may be pleasing to the Lord our God.

Pray brothers and sisters

When the priest asks the people to pray that "my sacrifice and yours" may be acceptable we are reminded that the priest acts in the person of Christ.

The Prayer over the Offerings

Just as the Collect Prayer closes the Introductory Rites, so the Prayer over the Gifts concludes the rite of preparation. In ancient times this prayer was the only formulary used at the presentation of the gifts. These prayers ask that the gifts placed upon the altar will become for us the bread of life and pledge of eternal salvation.

The Eucharistic Prayer

"Always and for everything giving thanks in the name of our Lord Jesus Christ."

(Ephesians 5: 20)

Lift up your hearts

"The Eucharistic Prayer is the centre and summit of the entire celebration. The different Eucharistic Prayers contained in the Missal have been handed down to us by the Church's living Tradition and are noteworthy for their inexhaustible theological and spiritual richness." (Pope Benedict XVI)

Let us give thanks to the Lord our God

We give thanks to the Father for the gifts of creation and his providential care. The wonders that God has done for us through his Son, Jesus Christ our Lord call for a "chorus of exultant praise". We are, therefore, invited to join our voices with the Angels and the whole heavenly host to sing the praises of God.

Holy, Holy, Holy Lord God of hosts. Heaven and earth are full of your glory

This hymn to the infinite holiness of God is found in the Eucharistic Prayers of both the Western and Eastern Church since the fourth century. "Holy, holy, holy is the Lord of hosts; the whole earth is full of his glory." (*Isaiah* 6: 1-5) As Jesus entered Jerusalem, the crowds that went before him were shouting, "Hosanna to the Son of David! Blessed is he who comes in the name of the Lord! Hosanna in the highest!" (*Matthew* 21: 9)

The Eucharistic Prayer developed its form very early in the history of the Church. We can recognise it in this description given by St Cyril of Jerusalem (313-386).

"We beg God to grant peace to all the Churches, to give harmony to the whole world, to assist all those who are in need; we all pray for all these intentions and we offer this victim for them... and last of all we pray for our deceased holy forefathers and bishops and for all those who have lived among us. For we have a deep conviction that great help will be afforded those souls for whom prayers are offered while this holy and awesome victim is present.

"'From the rising of the sun to its setting, praised be the name of the Lord.' (*Psalm* 113:3) Make holy these gifts, we pray, by sending down your Spirit upon them".

The Church invokes the power of the Holy Spirit that the gifts offered by human hands be consecrated, that is, become Christ's Body and Blood, and that the spotless Victim to be received in Communion, be for the salvation of those who will partake of it.

For on the night he was betrayed he took bread, and said, "This is my Body"

"These words that Jesus spoke at the Last Supper are repeated every time that the Eucharistic Sacrifice is renewed. They lead us in spirit to the Upper Room; they make us relive the spiritual atmosphere of that night when, celebrating Easter with his followers, the Lord mystically anticipated the sacrifice that was to be consummated the following day on the Cross. The Institution of the Eucharist thus appears to us as an anticipation and acceptance, on Jesus's part, of his death. St Ephrem the Syrian writes on this topic: "during the Supper Jesus sacrificed himself; on the Cross he was sacrificed by others". (Pope Benedict XVI)

"The bread which we break, is it not a communion in the body of Christ? Because there is one bread, we who are many are one body, for we all partake of the one bread." (1 *Corinthians* 10:16-17)

He gave the chalice to his disciples, saying: "Take this, all of you, and drink from it, for this is the chalice of my blood".

"With these words Jesus presents himself as the true and definitive sacrifice, in which was fulfilled the expiation of sins which, in the Old Testament rites, was never fully completed. Our Lord Jesus Christ says that his Blood 'is poured out for many' with a comprehensible reference to the songs of the Servant of God that are found in the Book of Isaiah. With the addition 'blood of the Covenant' Jesus also makes clear that through his death the prophesy of the new Covenant is fulfilled, based on the fidelity and infinite love of the Son made man. An alliance that therefore is stronger than all humanity's sins.

"It was during the Last Supper that he made this new Covenant with his disciples and humanity, with his own Blood, which became the 'Blood of the New Covenant'". (Pope Benedict XVI)

Do this in memory of me

The Church, fulfilling the command that she received from Christ the Lord through the Apostles, keeps the memorial of Christ, recalling especially his blessed Passion, glorious Resurrection, and Ascension into heaven.

The mystery of faith

"For as often as you eat this bread and drink the cup, you proclaim the death of the Lord until he comes."

(1 Corinthians 11:26)

We celebrate the memorial of the saving Passion of your Son, his wondrous Resurrection and Ascension into heaven, we offer you in thanksgiving this holy and living sacrifice.

"The prayers and rites of the Eucharistic sacrifice revive the whole history of salvation continuously before the eyes of our soul, in the course of the liturgical cycle and make us enter its significance ever more deeply." (St Teresa Benedicta of the Cross)

To us, also, your servants

In this very memorial, the Church, gathered here, offers in the Holy Spirit the spotless Victim to the Father. The Church's intention, however, is that the faithful not only offer this spotless Victim but also learn to offer themselves, and so day by day to be consummated, through Christ the Mediator, into unity with God and with each other, so that at last God may be all in all.

For our Pope and bishop

"The whole Catholic Church spread throughout the earth."

(St Polycarp)

Prayer for the whole Church was important for the first Christian communities. St Polycarp shortly before his death in the year 156, prayed aloud "for all who were know to him and for the whole Catholic Church spread throughout the earth".

With all the Saints, on whose constant intercession we rely for unfailing help

The Eucharist is always celebrated in communion with the entire Church, of heaven as well as of earth, and the offering is made for her and for all her members, living and dead, who have been called to participate in the redemption and the salvation purchased by Christ's Body and Blood.

Remember also our brothers and sisters who have fallen asleep in the hope of the resurrection

It is a holy and wholesome thought to pray for the dead that they may be released from their sins.

"For if we have been united with him in a death like his, we shall certainly be united with him in a resurrection like his." (*Romans* 6:5)

Through him, and with him, and in him

"For of him, and by him, and in him, are all things: to him be glory for ever. Amen."

(Romans 11: 36)

The Communion Rite

The Lord's Prayer

"The Lord's Prayer is truly the summary of the whole Gospel."
(Tertullian)

In response to his disciples' request, "Lord, teach us to pray" (*Luke* 11:1), Jesus commanded them to pray the great Christian prayer, the Our Father.

"The Lord's Prayer is the most perfect of prayers... In it we ask, not only for all the things we can rightly desire, but also in the sequence that they should be desired. This prayer not only teaches us to ask for things, but also in what order we should desire them." (St Thomas Aquinas)

For the kingdom, the power and the glory are yours now and for ever

The acclamation "For the kingdom, the power and the glory are yours, now and forever," takes up "the first three petitions to our Father: the glorification of his name, the coming of his reign, and the power of his saving will. But these prayers are now proclaimed as adoration and thanksgiving, as in the liturgy of heaven. The ruler of this world has mendaciously attributed to himself the three titles of kingship, power, and glory. Christ, the Lord, restores them to his Father and our Father, until he hands over the kingdom to him when the mystery of salvation will be brought to its completion and God will be all in all." (*Catechism* 2855)

Lord Jesus Christ, look not on our sins, but on the faith of your Church

"Peace I leave with you; my peace I give to you" (*John* 14:27). "Peace makers who sow in peace reap a harvest of righteousness." (*James* 4:17-18)

The sign of peace

"May the peace of the Risen Christ reign in your hearts, for as members of the one body you have been called to that peace!" (*Colossians* 3:15)

The altar is kissed because it has been consecrated by the invocation of the Holy Spirit. The Gospel book is kissed because through the power of the spirit Christ is present in the assembly when his word is proclaimed. The kiss of peace is given as a sign of reverence to our neighbour because, as St Paul tells us, our body is the temple of the Holy Spirit.

The peace of the Lord be with you always

"It should be kept in mind that nothing is lost when the sign of peace is marked by a sobriety which preserves the proper spirit of the celebration, as, for example, when it is restricted to one's immediate neighbours." (*Sacramentum Caritatis* n. 49)

The Fraction, the Breaking of the Bread

"They recognised him in the breaking of bread."

(Luke 24:35).

"The 'breaking of bread' as the Eucharist was called in earliest times, has always been at the centre of the Church's life. Through it Christ makes present within time the mystery of his death and Resurrection. In it he is received in person as the 'living bread come down from heaven', and with him we receive the pledge of eternal life and a foretaste of the eternal banquet of the heavenly Jerusalem." (Pope St John Paul II)

May this mingling of the Body and Blood of our Lord Jesus Christ bring eternal life to us who receive it.

The mingling of the two Species is a direct preparation for the reception of the Body and Blood of the Lord and reminds us that we are destined to participate in the divinity and immortality of Christ won for us by his Passion, death and Resurrection.

Lamb of God, you take away the sins of the world, have mercy on us

John the Baptist looked at Jesus and pointed him out as the "Lamb of God, who takes away the sin of the world".

By doing so, he reveals that Jesus is at the same time the suffering Servant who silently allows himself to be led to the slaughter and who bears the sin of the multitudes, and also the Paschal Lamb, the symbol of Israel's redemption at the first Passover. Christ's whole life expresses his mission: "to serve, and to give his life as a ransom for many".

Behold the Lamb of God, behold him who takes away the sins of the world

With these words John the Baptist pointed out the Lord's Anointed when he came, and John continues his mission to point out Christ to us until the Lord comes again at the end of time.

Lord, I am not worthy that you should enter under my roof, but only say the word and my soul shall be healed

At this most sacred moment of Communion the Church puts on our lips, not the words of a great saint or mystic, but those of a pagan soldier who showed great faith and trust in the Lord and took that vital first step of inviting him into his life. (See *Matthew* 8: 5-13)

Holy Communion may be received in the hand or on the tongue. St Cyril of Jerusalem told his congregation, "When you approach make your left hand a throne for your right hand, since the latter is to receive the King".

The Body of Christ. Amen

"Not without reason do you say 'Amen', for you acknowledge in your heart that you are receiving the body of Christ. When you present yourself, the priest says to you, 'the body of Christ.', and you reply 'Amen' that is, 'it is so'. Let the heart persevere in what the tongue confesses." (St Ambrose)

"Come to communion… It is true that you are not worthy of it, but you need it." (The Curé d'Ars, St John Mary Vianney)

The Concluding Rites

The Blessing and Dismissal

"The love that we celebrate in the sacrament is not something we can keep to ourselves. By its very nature it demands to be shared with all. What the world needs is God's love; it needs to encounter Christ and to believe in him. The Eucharist is thus the source and summit not only of the Church's life, but also of her mission: 'an authentically Eucharistic Church is a missionary Church.'

"We too must tell our brothers and sisters with conviction: 'That which we have seen and heard we proclaim also to you, so that you may have fellowship with us'. Truly, nothing is more beautiful than to know Christ and to make him known to others." (Pope Benedict XVI)

Go in peace, glorifying the Lord by your life

"Receiving the Bread of Life, the disciples of Christ ready themselves to undertake with the strength of the Risen Lord and his Spirit the tasks which await them in their ordinary life. For the faithful who have understood the meaning of what they have done, the Eucharistic celebration does not stop at the church door. Like the first witnesses of the Resurrection, Christians who gather each Sunday to experience and proclaim the presence of the Risen Lord are called to evangelise and bear witness in their daily lives. Given this, the Prayer after Communion and the Concluding

Rite - the Final Blessing and the Dismissal - need to be better valued and appreciated, so that all who have shared in the Eucharist may come to a deeper sense of the responsibility which is entrusted to them. Once the assembly disperses, Christ's disciples return to their everyday surroundings with the commitment to make their whole life a gift, a spiritual sacrifice pleasing to God. They feel indebted to their brothers and sisters because of what they have received in the celebration, not unlike the disciples of Emmaus who, once they had recognised the Risen Christ 'in the breaking of the bread' felt the need to return immediately to share with their brothers and sisters the joy of meeting the Lord." (Pope St John Paul II)

The priest venerates the altar with a kiss. After making a profound bow with the ministers, he withdraws.

Conclusion

Nothing can replace reading, meditating and praying the texts of the liturgy. May this simple guide help the reader to enter more deeply into the celebration of the Mystery of Faith.

THE HEART OF CHRISTIANITY

Unanswered questions

Many people find it hard to believe in a loving God. They doubt his existence altogether, or their experience of suffering and human tragedy make them doubt his love. Scientists seem to be solving the great puzzles of the universe, and psychologists seek to unlock the deepest mysteries of the human heart.

But there are some questions that don't go away.

- What caused the whole universe to exist in the first place?
- Why is there so much suffering in the world?
- What is the meaning of human life?
- What is the point of my own individual life?
- Is there such a thing as life after death?

These are huge questions. You would be suspicious if someone claimed to answer them with any certainty. There is a limit, surely, to what we can discover for ourselves, and very often we need to admit that some questions are simply beyond human understanding.

God has not left us alone

The heart of Christianity, however, is the belief that God has spoken to us in human history, by sending us his Son.

He has not left us alone. He has revealed himself to us. We don't have to go round in circles trying to solve everything ourselves. He has come to our help.

The idea that Christians claim to know the truth about God will sound arrogant or even fundamentalist to many people. But in fact there is a kind of humility behind this claim. It's not that Christians, as people, are special - far from it. It's that they have been given the most extraordinary gift: the knowledge of Jesus Christ. And their desire is simply to share that gift with others. It's Jesus himself who taught that he is the Way to God, and the Truth, and the Life.

The Christian message

What, then, is the Christian message? It is this: that God is love. His love created and sustains the whole universe. His love brings into being every human life. We were meant to live in peace with God and with each other, but this peace was broken through hatred and sin.

In the fulness of time, God sent his only Son, Jesus Christ, to be our Saviour. He came into the world to reveal the love and mercy of God, and to lead us to the Father. Through him we can find peace with God and with each other. His death on the Cross brings us forgiveness. His Resurrection on the third day, and his Ascension to heaven, give us the hope of an astonishing new life. And the gift of the Holy Spirit allows us to share in that life even now on this earth, through faith and through belonging to the Church.

You may not be convinced by these ideas. But at least you can see that the heart of Christianity is not a theory or a programme but a person: Jesus Christ. A person we can come to know, above all through faith.

An invitation to believe

Faith is a gift. We can only believe in Jesus Christ if the Holy Spirit helps us to believe. At the same time, faith is a step that we can choose to take - it is a personal decision.

In any human relationship there are moments when we need to trust and to make a commitment - despite our uncertainties. It's the same with God. He calls us to trust him and to reach out to him.

Faith changes everything. It transforms our life, our relationships, our hopes, our love.

Don't be afraid of taking a step in faith. You might do this in different ways. You might speak to a Christian friend about their faith, and find out what it means to them.

You might read some of the Bible, or find a Christian book or website that could help you. You might visit a Christian church, and appreciate the beauty and serenity of the building. You might speak to a priest, and put some questions to him, or find out if there is a group for enquirers in a local church that you could join.

An invitation to pray

The simplest and most important way of taking a step in faith is to pray. Don't be afraid to open your heart to God in prayer, however nervous or uncertain you feel. He always responds, even if it is in quiet and unexpected ways. Say to him, out loud if it helps, a simple phrase like: "Lord, help me". "God, have mercy on me". "Jesus, I believe in you". Or simply, "Lord, I want to believe, help my lack of faith". If it is helpful, you could pray with the words of the Lord's Prayer, the Our Father, which Jesus gave us. Or if this is all too much, you could just sit in silence, with the intention in your heart that God would guide you and be with you.

To pray in any of these ways is like opening a door. It allows God to work in your life and reveal himself more and more. Faith is not an irrational leap in the dark, it is a response to the love of God. And perhaps, in the depths of your heart, he is calling you, even if you are not sure how to interpret that call. What matters is that we try to respond. It was Jesus who said, "Ask, and it will be given unto you; search, and you will find; knock, and the door will be opened to you."

The Church

Eventually, if you come closer to Christ in faith, this desire will bring you to the Church. The Church is the community that Jesus himself founded, so that his followers would always have a spiritual home to live in, a family to belong to. This community is found today in its fulness in the Catholic Church.

In the Church we receive the life of Christ in the sacraments; we come to know him through the inspired words of the Bible; we hear his teaching through the bishops and the Pope; and we share in the great tradition of Christian faith that stretches back through the centuries.

The Church is a rock that Christ never abandons, despite the sins and weaknesses of her members. It is a spiritual home that will always be a place of safety and security, a place where we can rejoice in the gifts of the Holy Spirit and in the friendship of our fellow Christians.

The love of God

So whatever you feel about your own worth, never doubt that your life has a meaning. God created you for a purpose. He loves you and cares for you. And he is closer to you than you can imagine. You will never find true peace or lasting happiness without him. As St Augustine wrote:

"Lord, you have made us for yourself; and our hearts are restless until they rest in you".

Whatever your questions and doubts, don't be afraid to find out more about him and open your heart to him.

A Guide for Christian Living

The heart of Christ's moral and spiritual teaching is given in the Sermon on the Mount (in St Matthew's Gospel, chapters 5 to 7). This is an abridged version. It gives us a vision and guide for Christian living.

The Beatitudes

How blessed are the poor in spirit:
　　the kingdom of heaven is theirs.
Blessed are the gentle:
　　they shall have the earth as inheritance.
Blessed are those who mourn:
　　they shall be comforted.
Blessed are those who hunger and thirst
　　for uprightness: they shall have their fill.
Blessed are the merciful:
　　they shall have mercy shown them.
Blessed are the pure in heart:
　　they shall see God.
Blessed are the peacemakers:
　　they shall be recognised as children of God.
Blessed are those who are persecuted
　　in the cause of uprightness:
　　the kingdom of heaven is theirs.
Blessed are you when people abuse you and persecute you and speak of all kinds of calumny against you falsely on my account. Rejoice and be glad, for your reward will be great in heaven.

You are light for the world. A city built on a hill-top cannot be hidden. No one lights a lamp to put it under a tub; they put it on the lamp-stand where it shines for everyone in the house. In the same way your light must shine in people's sight, so that, seeing your good works, they may give praise to your Father in heaven.

The Commandments

Do not imagine that I have come to abolish the Law or the Prophets. I have come not to abolish but to complete them.

You have heard how it was said: You shall not kill. But I say this to you, anyone who is angry with a brother will answer for it. If you are bringing your offering to the altar and there remember that your brother has something against you, leave your offering there before the altar, go and be reconciled with your brother first, and then come back and present your offering.

You have heard how it was said: You shall not commit adultery. But I say this to you, if a man looks at a woman lustfully, he has already committed adultery with her in his heart. If your right eye should be your downfall, tear it out and throw it away; for it will do you less harm to lose one part of yourself than to have your whole body thrown into hell.

It has also been said: Anyone who divorces his wife must give her a writ of dismissal. But I say this to you, everyone who divorces his wife, except for the case of an illicit marriage, makes her an adulteress; and anyone who marries a divorced woman commits adultery.

You have heard how it was said: You must not break your oath, but must fulfil your oaths to the Lord. But I say this to you, do not swear at all. All you need say is "Yes" if you mean yes, "No" if you mean no.

You have heard how it was said: Eye for eye and tooth for tooth. But I say this to you; offer no resistance to the wicked. If anyone hits you on the right cheek, offer him the other as well; if someone wishes to go to law with you to get your tunic, let him have your cloak as well. And if anyone requires you to go one mile, go two miles with him. Give to anyone who asks you, and if anyone wants to borrow, do not turn away.

You have heard how it was said: You will love your neighbour and hate your enemy. But I say this to you, love your enemies and pray for those who persecute you; so that you may be children of your Father in heaven, for he causes his sun to rise on the bad as well as the good, and sends down rain to fall on the upright and the wicked alike. For if you love those who love you, what reward will you get? You must therefore set no bounds to your love, just as your heavenly Father sets none to his.

Humility and prayer

Be careful not to parade your uprightness in public to attract attention; otherwise you will lose all reward from your Father in heaven. When you give alms, your left hand must not know what your right is doing; your almsgiving must be secret, and your Father who sees all that is done in secret will reward you.

When you pray, go to your private room, shut yourself in, and so pray to your Father who is in that secret place, and your Father who sees all that is done in secret will reward you.

In your prayers do not babble as the gentiles do, for they think that by using many words they will make themselves heard. Your Father knows what you need before you ask him.

So you should pray like this:

Our Father in heaven, may your name be held holy, your kingdom come, your will be done, on earth as in heaven. Give us today our daily bread. And forgive us our debts, as we have forgiven those who are in debt to us. And do not put us to the test, but save us from the Evil One.

When you are fasting, put scent on your head and wash your face, so that no one will know you are fasting except your Father who sees all that is done in secret.

Trust in God

Do not store up treasures for yourselves on earth, where moth and woodworm destroy them and thieves can break in and steal. But store up treasures for yourselves in heaven. For wherever your treasure is, there will your heart be too.

No one can be the slave of two masters. You cannot be the slave of God and of money.

That is why I am telling you not to worry about your life and what you are to eat, nor about your body and what you are to wear. Look at the birds in the sky. They do not sow or reap or gather into barns; yet your heavenly Father feeds them. Are you not worth much more than they are?

Can any of you, however much you worry, add one single cubit to your span of life?

So do not worry. Set your hearts on his kingdom first, and on God's saving justice, and all these other things will be given you as well. So do not worry about tomorrow; tomorrow will take care of itself. Each day has enough trouble of its own.

Do not judge, and you will not be judged; because the judgements you give are the judgements you will get. Why do you observe the splinter in your brother's eye and never notice the great log in your own? Hypocrite! Take the log out of your own eye first, and then you will see clearly enough to take the splinter out of your brother's eye.

Ask, and it will be given unto you; search, and you will find; knock, and the door will be opened to you. Everyone who asks receives; everyone who searches finds; everyone who knocks will have the door opened. Is there anyone among you who would hand his son a stone when he asked for bread? If you, then, evil as you are, know how to give your children what is good, how much more will your Father in heaven give good things to those who ask him!

Bearing Good Fruit

So always treat others as you would like them to treat you; that is the Law and the Prophets. Enter by the narrow gate, since the road that leads to destruction is wide and spacious, and many take it; but it is a narrow gate and a hard road that leads to life, and only a few find it.

Beware of false prophets who come to you disguised as sheep but underneath are ravenous wolves. You will be able to tell them by their fruits. A sound tree produces good fruit but a rotten tree bad fruit.

It is not anyone who says to me, "Lord, Lord," who will enter the kingdom of heaven, but the person who does the will of my Father in heaven. Therefore, everyone who listens to these words of mine and acts on them will be like a sensible man who built his house on rock. Rain came down, floods rose, gales blew and hurled themselves against that house, and it did not fall: it was founded on rock.

What is the Catholic Faith?

It's impossible to summarise the Catholic faith in a few hundred words. This chapter will simply give you an idea of the main areas of Catholic belief, and perhaps encourage you to look into some of them more deeply.

God

There are good reasons for believing in God. Faith is not a superstition or an irrational leap. The existence of the universe points to some kind of creative power that brought it into being and sustains it. The underlying laws of nature cannot have arisen just by chance.

So there is no fundamental conflict between science and religion. Science asks the question:

- How do things work in the world?

Religion asks different questions:

- Why is there any world at all?
- What is my place within it?

The human person

Many animals are remarkably skilled and inventive. But human beings have a distinctive place in creation. Our openness to truth and beauty, our freedom and moral conscience, cannot be explained in purely natural terms.

They are spiritual gifts that reflect something of God's own likeness and give us a special dignity.

But human life is fragile and often marked by suffering.

We catch glimpses of evil in the world and in our own hearts. We have an intuition that things are not as they were meant to be, and there is a longing in the depths of our hearts for a happiness which is not of this world.

Jesus

God did not leave us alone. He has revealed himself to us. He spoke first to the Jewish people, his chosen ones, through the Law and the prophets. He taught them to wait for the promised Saviour. When the time was right, about two thousand years ago, he fulfilled his promises by sending his own Son to be born of the Virgin Mary in Bethlehem.

Jesus Christ is the Son of God, the only Saviour of the world. He is a human being like us, but without sin. And he is the all-powerful and eternal God, infinite in knowledge and love.

Salvation

Jesus transformed people's lives by his teaching and his miracles. He reached out to them with God's healing and forgiveness. His greatest act of love was to offer his life for us in sacrifice, in obedience to the Father. He let himself experience the depths of human suffering, even to being crucified. His death on the Cross brings us forgiveness and reconciliation. It means that nothing has to separate us from the love of God in Christ.

On the third day, God raised Jesus from the dead. Jesus then revealed himself plainly to his followers, and convinced them that he had truly risen from the dead. By ascending to heaven in his glorified humanity he showed that our goal is to be with God for all eternity.

After his Ascension, Jesus sent the Holy Spirit to his followers so that they could share in his divine life and proclaim it to others. In this way he revealed the mystery of the Holy Trinity: that within the unity of God there is a communion of Divine Persons - the Father, the Son, and the Holy Spirit - equal in majesty and glory.

Faith

Faith is our wholehearted response to the love of Christ, when we believe in him and entrust our lives to him. Through faith and baptism our sins are forgiven and we are reborn as God's adopted children. We share in God's own life, and the Holy Trinity comes to dwell within our souls.

Faith is a pure gift, given by the Holy Spirit. But faith is also something that we must freely choose, by accepting Jesus as our Saviour and believing in his teaching.

The Church

Faith is never lived alone. Jesus gathered his followers together into a new family called the Church, founded on the twelve Apostles. This community would be a sign of his continuing presence in the world, and a place where people could share in the new life Jesus had won for them.

Jesus gave his Church a way of life that is handed on in its Tradition. He gave it the inspired words of the Holy Scriptures, in the Bible. This community that Jesus founded continues today in its fulness in the Catholic Church. The Pope and the Catholic bishops, despite their weaknesses, continue the work of the first Apostles as shepherds and teachers of the Church.

The sacraments

Our lives are transformed by the seven sacraments that Christ gave to his Church. A sacrament is a sacred ritual that helps us to see the reality of salvation, and allows that reality to change our lives. The sacraments give us a share in God's own life through the gift of the Holy Spirit and through our response of faith.

Baptism and Confirmation unite us with the death and Resurrection of Jesus and make us Christians. Marriage and Ordination give us specific vocations. Reconciliation ('Confession') and Anointing bring us forgiveness and healing. In the Mass, the Holy Eucharist, we share in the once-for-all sacrifice of Christ on Calvary. Through the power of the Holy Spirit, with Christ and with the whole Church, we worship the Father. And in Holy Communion we receive Christ himself as food and drink.

Love

A living faith involves a commitment to follow Christ and to do the Father's will. The heart of Christian morality is the twin commandment to love God and to love our neighbour. It is to love as Christ himself loved.

Christ gives us his own moral teaching in the New Testament, which fulfils the teaching of the Old Testament. He continues to guide us by means of the moral teaching of the Catholic Church in every generation. By living a faithful Christian life we help to build God's kingdom of peace and justice in this world, and we witness to the power of Christ's love in our lives. If we fail through weakness or sin, we can turn to the inexhaustible mercy of God.

Prayer

In prayer we lift our hearts and minds to God. We praise him and thank him. We ask for his forgiveness and help, for ourselves and for others. All Christian prayer is made "in the name of Jesus". This reminds us that we can only reach the Father's heart through Christ, in the power of the Holy Spirit. Christians worship only God, but they also honour the saints and the angels and call on their help - especially the Virgin Mary.

Hope

Death is a frightening mystery that awaits us all. When we die, our spiritual souls will come into the presence of God. We will see the whole truth of our lives. Those who believe in Christ, who freely choose to accept the mercy and salvation he offers, will enter heaven - even though some may need to pass through the purification of purgatory. Those who reject Christ, who freely choose to turn away from the mercy and salvation he offers, will be condemned - condemned by their own actions and choices. For them there will be no possibility of life with God. This is the tragedy of hell.

At the end of time, when Christ comes again, our bodies will share in the Resurrection. God will reveal the hidden purposes of his creation, and reconcile all things in Christ. The just will live in the presence of God for all eternity. The hope of heaven gives us joy even in the sufferings of this life, and gives us reason to keep close to Christ through lives of faith and love.

HOW TO BECOME
A CATHOLIC

Thinking of becoming Catholic?

People from all kinds of backgrounds, and for all kinds of different reasons, express an interest in knowing more about the Catholic faith. You may be engaged, or married, to a Catholic; you may belong to another Christian denomination, perhaps baptised or not, or a member of another religion, or none. You may be searching for the answers to some sincere and important questions about life.

What does the Catholic Church claim to be?

The Roman Catholic Church claims that it is the visible community established by Jesus Christ, and built up by his first disciples, the Apostles - we can trace our life back two thousand years to his life on earth and to his teachings and ministry. It is God's will that all men and women should encounter the Christian message, so the Catholic Church is at heart a missionary organisation, seeking all the time to encourage people to become Catholics. So, in the first place, Catholics will welcome that you are considering this step in your life by reading this.

How do I get started?

Personal contact is often better than reading a booklet, so the first thing you should do is speak to a priest at a Catholic Church near where you live or work. He will be able to talk to you about what is involved in becoming a Catholic; he can talk with you about your life and background, and what it is that has prompted you to make this enquiry.

How do I find out some basic information?

If you don't know where the nearest church is, you'll find that Catholic churches are usually listed in telephone directories. Most Catholic parishes will have a website giving details of Mass times and other basic information. If you can find a church near where you live or work, the best way to be introduced to the Church's life is to go to Mass on a Sunday or a weekday and look at parish newsletters or magazines so you can see something of local Catholic life; there should also be copies of Catholic newspapers which tell you of the life of the Church in the rest of the country and the world.

How does the learning process begin... and end?

Sometimes the priest will offer to help you consider becoming a Catholic by individual sessions with him, so that you can learn about what the Catholic Church teaches and discern God's will for you. This is an important time and it doesn't pay to rush, no matter how enthusiastic you may feel. Alternatively, instruction may be given in groups, with other people in the same position as yourself, which might be called by various names - RCIA (which stands for the Rite of Christian Initiation of Adults), Journey of Faith, or something similar. These groups meet over a period of months. Usually adults who wish to become Catholics do so at Easter, during the late night Mass on the Saturday evening before Easter, the Easter Vigil - the greatest feast in the Catholic calendar!

What other things will I need to do to be baptised?

If you have never been baptised, that is "christened", then if you proceed you will be baptised as an adult and confirmed.

If you have been baptised in another Christian church whose rite of baptism the Catholic Church recognises as valid the Catholic community accepts that baptism, and welcomes your experience of Christianity in that church.

You cannot be baptised again, so you are confirmed and "received into full communion" with the Catholic Church, often with others who have to be baptised as adults. In some parishes those who need to be baptised are prepared separately from those who have already been baptised in another church; in others everybody is prepared together.

Catholics, normally as children and as they grow up, receive several sacraments:

Baptism (becoming members of God's Church); the Eucharist (receiving Our Lord as the Bread of Life); Reconciliation, also known as Confession (receiving the forgiveness of sins); and Confirmation (receiving the strength to be soldiers for Christ). Depending on your present situation (baptised or un-baptised etc), you may be introduced to all of these along this new journey.

Is there anyone else who can help me through all this?

Usually the whole church community in the parish is invited to support you and an individual layperson will help you as a godparent or sponsor during your preparation period. Usually those who are being prepared are supported in special ceremonies in the months leading up to their becoming Catholics in the local church and the cathedral: this emphasises that when you become a Catholic you are not simply taking an individual step in your life - you are also becoming part of the wider family of the Catholic Church in the local area and throughout the world.

What if I'm not sure about something... or everything?

In these settings, either individually with a priest or in a group, you will have the chance to ask questions about what you are being taught, to share any doubts or problems you may have, and to talk about your own life history and the influences in your life. People will also be able to suggest things you can read: you should certainly get hold of a good modern Catholic edition of the Bible, such as the New Jerusalem Bible, and the *Catechism of the Catholic Church*, which explains all the main Catholic beliefs in a comprehensive way.

How else can I help myself?

In addition to this, you might find it helpful to talk to other people you know who are Catholics; they might be friends, members of your family, or people you work with.

Being a Catholic isn't always easy, and like the Gospel itself, is challenging: so ask them to be honest with you!

God encounters us in many different ways in our lives, and personal contact with other people is a good way of learning about something.

What are the consequences?

As a Catholic you become part of a worldwide community of believers, and of a local parish; you will want to familiarise yourself with Catholic moral and social teaching; you will be responsible as a parent for educating your children in the Catholic faith. Above all as you grow in faith, you will be a true "light of Christ".

And what about the future?

The journey doesn't end with confirmation. As Catholics we should pray every day, take part in the Mass every Sunday and Holy Day of Obligation, live the seasons and feasts of the Church's life, receive the sacraments and live a life of Christian charity towards our fellow man. Christ invited us to deny ourselves, take up our cross and follow him. You are special and unique in the sight of God. He wants the best for you and is leading you to himself. As you reflect on how to become a Catholic, try to be open to God's will.

Why signs and images?

A Catholic Church, whether old or new, will always be a building rich in signs and symbolism, and likely to contain objects and images not readily understandable to all visitors. However, we know that through our senses we engage with the world and grow in knowledge and so we depend on sight, hearing, touch, smell and taste. The Catholic Church makes use of all five senses to help us grow in knowledge of God and our faith, by way of "sacramentals" - these are symbols and images designed to help us in our relationship with God, and not simply "decoration".

The Sanctuary

The sanctuary is the most important area in the church, within which the priest celebrates the Mass and leads the services. It will usually be raised up a little, or in some other way separated from the rest of the building, while clearly still a part of it.

The Tabernacle

This is the most important object in the building - the living heart of a Catholic Church. The tabernacle is a shrine, usually made of precious metal and often veiled with a coloured cloth. It most often stands in the sanctuary, or perhaps in a small chapel of its own, set aside for private prayer. The tabernacle contains the Blessed Sacrament, the bread consecrated by the priest at Mass which is transformed into the Body of Christ. It is reserved in the tabernacle so that Holy Communion can be taken to the sick, but also so that people can pray in the presence of Jesus, who we believe remains there, body, blood, soul and divinity, under the appearance of bread. Near the tabernacle you will always see a lamp burning - symbolising the living presence of Jesus in the Blessed Sacrament.

The Altar

The altar will always be the most prominent object within the sanctuary, the holy table on which the sacrifice of the Mass is offered. Traditionally, an altar which has been consecrated (specially blessed by the bishop) is made of stone and contains relics of the saints - a practice which goes back to the earliest centuries of Christianity. Because the body and blood of Christ will rest here during Mass, the altar is treated with particular reverence: it is covered with a white cloth, and candles are placed on or near it. The priest will kiss it at the beginning and end of Mass, and it may be honoured with incense.

The Ambo or Lectern

Often placed within or close to the sanctuary, from here the Word of God (Scripture) is proclaimed during the Mass and other liturgies. If the altar is the 'first table', the ambo is a 'second table', of the word. Homilies, sermons and prayers are often given from the ambo, which is usually made of wood or stone, and can be elegantly decorated or covered, and treated with reverence.

The Font

The font is the place where infants (and occasionally adults) receive baptism. It can be located in a separate part of the church (called a baptistery), or may be found in or near the sanctuary.

Paschal Candle

Often near the font, this very large decorated candle is placed on a high stand: a new paschal candle is blessed each year at the Easter Vigil, and is lit throughout the Easter season and afterwards for every baptism and funeral - a powerful symbol of Jesus Christ, Light of the World and our hope of eternal life.

Aumbry

Near the font there may also be an aumbry, a special cupboard containing the holy oils used for baptisms, confirmations and anointing the sick.

Holy Water

This is another reminder of baptism which is found in stoups, or bowls, near the doors of a Catholic Church - on entering we make the Sign of the Cross with the holy water, which has been blessed by the priest, and can also be taken away for use in people's private devotion at home.

Crucifix or Cross

Another important image in the church is the crucifix which hangs somewhere near the altar: the image of Jesus on the Cross reminds us of his supreme, loving sacrifice which is represented for us at every celebration of the Mass.

The Sacred Heart

A familiar image of Jesus which will be found in almost every Catholic Church is the Sacred Heart, showing Jesus displaying his wounded heart - another reminder of his wonderful love. Devotion to the heart of Jesus is very old, but is especially associated with St Margaret Mary Alacoque, who lived in the seventeenth century.

Stations of the Cross

These fourteen pictures, or carvings, which can be elaborate or very simple, depict the final journey of Jesus to Calvary, from his judgement by Pilate to his burial in the tomb. Usually set on the walls, Catholics use this set of images in their private prayers or sometimes - especially during Lent - at a public service.

Images of the Mother of Jesus

Catholics venerate Mary as Mother of God, and in a special way as the spiritual mother of all Christians. In honouring Mary we honour her Son, and we believe that she will always pray for his disciples. Catholics worship God alone, but we honour Mary as a person uniquely close to Jesus Christ. Thus we can be sure of finding in any Catholic church a statue, or at least a picture, of the Blessed Virgin Mary (Our Lady) often depicted holding the infant Jesus.

Images of the Saints

Usually churches will contain images of certain other saints. Catholics believe that the thousands of Catholic saints are our friends, and seeing their image inspires us to be like them. The choice for a particular church will depend on its history, location and dedication, and other special circumstances. A saint very often depicted is St Joseph, the foster-father of Jesus: either holding the Christ Child, or sometimes with a carpenter's tools. Others are St Anthony, St Patrick, St Jude and St Thérèse of Lisieux.

Vestments and Colours

During Mass the priest wears special vestments. These derive from the clothing commonly worn by people during the first centuries of Christianity. Secular fashion changed, but the Church kept to the old style. Thus it was that clothing once common to all became the distinctive dress of the clergy. The colour of these vestments, and very often the veil of the tabernacle and other hangings, will vary according to the season of the Church's year.

- Purple, a colour of penance and expectation, is worn during Advent and Lent. It is also appropriately worn at funerals, when we pray for the deceased on their final journey to God.

- White, a joyful colour, is worn at Christmas and Easter, and for feasts of Our Lady and many saints.

- Red, colour of fire and blood, is worn on feasts of the Holy Spirit and in commemorating the suffering of Jesus and his martyrs.

- Green, symbolic of life and growth, is worn on the Sundays in Ordinary Time.

- Rose-coloured vestments may be worn to mark the middle Sundays of Advent and Lent.

- Black, the colour of mourning, remains an option at funerals and for All Souls' Day (2 November), though not so common now.

- Gold and silver vestments may be worn on very important feasts, such as Easter and Christmas.

The Liturgy

At Mass, there will be a further use of symbols: the use of candles, incense and bodily gestures (kneeling, bowing, genuflecting etc.) involve all the senses in our act of worship and reverence.

If you are becoming a Catholic, or discovering these things for the first time, they can seem confusing. Time taken to learn about them will help you to appreciate them more as an appropriate response to the unfathomable riches of our Christian faith.

HOW TO PRAY

"Teach us to pray"

Jesus's disciples said to him: "Lord, teach us to pray" (*Luke* 11:1). Today, too, many people find themselves asking the same thing. The Catholic Church has a wonderful tradition of prayer on which to draw. Unfortunately, many Catholics still see prayer as something complicated and difficult, or reserved for "professionals" (perhaps priests and religious sisters). This is the first myth to slay! Prayer is not complicated and it is meant for everyone. An early Christian poet, St Ephraem, wrote: "Birds fly, fish swim, people pray." Human beings are made to pray, because they are made for God.

Contemplative prayer

All prayer is valuable, even the most short and spontaneous, but the prayer that goes deepest, and truly touches the heart, is the form of prayer known as contemplative, or mental prayer. Again, the terminology can put people off: but it shouldn't. All prayer can be defined very simply - "conversation with God". In contemplative prayer the conversation is longer than usual, and to help prevent our minds wandering, we make use of a few basic rules. But the rules are very simple, and mental prayer can be made by anyone. As St Teresa of Avila said "Contemplative prayer is nothing else than a close sharing between friends; it means taking time frequently to be alone with him who we know loves us."

One form of prayer

Over the centuries, the Church and its saints have developed many different forms of mental prayer. The one outlined here is a simple one, a form made popular by St Francis de Sales in the seventeenth century, and used by millions of people ever since. St Francis aimed especially at the laity and people living in the secular world: he believed all were called to holiness, and all to prayer.

Finding a place to pray

Prayer is not complicated, but it needs patience and dedication. Finding appropriate surroundings is important: the great saints can pray anywhere and anytime, but most of us are not so fortunate! Try and find a quiet place where you won't be disturbed. If you have access to a church, that would be ideal - or the opportunity to pray before the Blessed Sacrament, even better. But a quiet room in your house will work just as well. It is also important to pray in an appropriate posture: sitting upright, or kneeling, helps to keep most people alert and attentive.

Giving time to prayer

How long should you pray for? As long as you can! It is obviously better to pray for five or ten minutes than not at all. That said, we do need to be generous with God, and practical - giving time to prayer allows us to listen as well as speak. Many people find it useful to give a set amount of time each day to prayer - "beginners" might like to start with, say, ten minutes. This may increase as time goes by. In time, some find half an hour or even an hour a day is what they grow to like and need. Set yourself a realistic target - and stick to it.

Don't be tempted to cut short your prayer because you may find it difficult at first - treat it as important, and persevere.

When to pray

What time of day is best for prayer? Well, we can pray at any time, morning, afternoon or evening. Realistically though, most people are more alert in the mornings. The later we leave our prayer, the more tired and distracted we may become.

The presence of God

When you come to pray, wherever it is, first remind yourself that God is there. Then consciously place yourself in his presence, and ask him to help you.

Lifting your mind

To come to prayer, we need to focus our minds on God. There are many ways to do this. You might read a brief passage from the Gospels, look at an icon or a crucifix, reflect on one of the Mysteries of the Rosary (the Rosary, incidentally, is itself an excellent form of mental prayer, if prayed reflectively). You can close your eyes. Be still and try to enter into your own heart, and quietly repeat a simple phrase, sincerely, such as "Lord Jesus, have mercy on me, help me". Don't be in a hurry. Once God has filled your thoughts - talk to him. Tell him you believe in him, hope in him, love him. Tell him your troubles and say sorry for your sins. This is prayer.

Distractions

Unless we are very focussed or very holy, our minds soon get distracted. From thinking of God, we soon find ourselves thinking of food, work, and our families. Don't be distracted by distractions. Even the saints suffered from them, and they are not important. If you find your thoughts have wandered, simply bring them back again (read another verse of the Gospel - fix your gaze on the icon - repeat your phrase). Distractions never entirely disappear, but they will grow less with practice. Don't be discouraged by them. They are quite normal. To pray can in this sense involve a bit of a battle.

Listening

In this way - thinking of, talking to, and loving God - our time of prayer will soon pass. But it is important that we listen too - a listening of the heart. If we treat God as a real friend - if we tell him our troubles, our difficulties and our temptations - then in prayer, he will show us the answers to all these questions, helping us to see things in a new perspective, with fresh understanding. Even the most insoluble problems can be resolved in prayer.

Conclusion

When our time of prayer is almost finished, there are three final things we should do.

1. Try and find something to "take away" with you - perhaps a word of Scripture, an idea or an image - something to remind you of your prayer throughout the day.

2. If appropriate, make a resolution: resolve to act as God has guided you in your prayer (and if you still feel a lack of guidance, ask God to show you the way forward).

3. Give thanks to God for this time of prayer, and ask him to remain with you always. You may want to end by saying a brief prayer of your own choice, such as the Our Father.

It is hard to write about prayer, because it is something that needs to be experienced. If you really want to learn to pray, then the only way to do it is to try. Set aside the time. Open your heart, and persevere - you will never look back, and you will never regret it.

Catholic Truth Society 40-46
Harleyford Road, London SE11 5AY

website: *CTSbooks.org*

CTS Code: D822

ISBN: 978 1 78469 186 8

Acknowledgements

This volume has been compiled from material previously published under the following titles: *Catholic Christianity,* first published 2013 by The Incorporated Catholic Truth Society; © 2013 The Incorporated Catholic Truth Society. *A Simple Guide to the Mass*, first published 2011 by The Incorporated Catholic Truth Society; Copyright © 2011 The Incorporated Catholic Truth Society and Dom Cuthbert Johnson OSB. *Marian Prayer Book,* first published 2012 by The Incorporated Catholic Truth Society, Compilation and design © 2012 The Incorporated Catholic Truth Society. Excerpts from the English translation of The Roman Missal © 2010, International Commission on English in the Liturgy Corporation (ICEL); excerpts from the English translation of The Liturgy of the Hours © 1974, ICEL; excerpts from the English translation of Holy Communion & Worship of the Eucharist outside Mass © 1974, ICEL; excerpt from the English translation of Rite of Penance © 1974, ICEL. All rights reserved. Latin text © Libreria Editrice Vaticana, Vatican City State, 2008. Concordat cum originali: Martin Foster (England and Wales). Permission granted for distribution in the dioceses of Scotland.